I0006608

Starting Struts 2

Written By:
Ian Roughley

© 2007 C4Media Inc
All rights reserved.

C4Media, Publisher of InfoQ.com.

This book is part of the InfoQ Enterprise Software Development series of books.

For information or ordering of this or other InfoQ books, please contact books@c4media.com.

No part of this publication may be reproduced, stored in a retrieval system or transmitted in any form or by any means, electronic, mechanical, photocopying, recoding, scanning or otherwise except as permitted under Sections 107 or 108 of the 1976 United States Copyright Act, without either the prior written permission of the Publisher.

Designations used by companies to distinguish their products are often claimed as trademarks. In all instances where C4Media Inc. is aware of a claim, the product names appear in initial Capital or ALL CAPITAL LETTERS. Readers, however, should contact the appropriate companies for more complete information regarding trademarks and registration.

Managing Editor: Diana Plesa
Cover art: Dixie Press
Composition: Dixie Press

Library of Congress Cataloguing-in-Publication Data:

ISBN: 978-1-4303-2033-3

Printed in the United States of America

Acknowledgements

This book would never have been possible without the tireless effort of all the developers of WebWork, XWork and Struts2. For my transition from open source user to open source developer, I would like to thank Patrick Lightbody and Jason Carreira.

To the technical reviewers – Don Brown, Philip Luppens and Rene Gielen – many thanks for providing the final adjustments on a moving target. I would like to acknowledge and thank both Jim Krygowski and James Walker for taking time out of their busy schedules to provide an impartial judgment on the continuity and content from a non-Struts2 perspective. With their assistance, the readers experience has improved without a doubt. I would like to thank Floyd Marinescu for his confidence, and for providing writing opportunities in both online and published formats.

I would also like to thank my remarkable wife LeAnn (a.k.a. STR Worldwide). Her continuing support and ongoing review and non-geek analysis of the manuscript has been invaluable.

Contents

INTRODUCTION   **1**

WHERE STRUTS2 FITS INTO THE WEB PARADIGM   **5**

Servlets   6
JSP and Scriptlet Development   6
Action-Based Frameworks   7
Component-Based Frameworks   7
The Great Equalizer – Ajax   8

CORE COMPONENTS   **11**

Configuration   12
Actions   19
Interceptors   25
Value Stack / OGNL   29
Result Types   31
Results / View Technologies   33

ARCHITECTURAL GOALS   **37**

Separation of Concerns   37
Loose Coupling   39
Testability   40
Modularization   44
Convention over Configuration   47

PRODUCTIVITY TIPS   **49**

Re-Using Action Configurations   50
Use Pattern Matching Wildcards in Configurations   51
Utilize Alternate URI Mapping Schemes   52
Know Interceptor Functionality   55
Use Provided Interceptor Stacks   58

Take Advantage of Result Types   60
Utilize Data Conversion   61
Utilize Tabular Data Entry Support   63
Expose Domain Models in the Action   65
Use Declarative Validation Where Possible   66
Move CRUD Operations into the same Action   70
Use Annotation Where Possible   73
Options for View Technologies   79
Know the Provided Tag Libraries and their Features 81
Customize UI Themes   87
Use Global Results for Common Outcomes   89
Manage Exception Handling Declaratively   89
Internationalization   92

INTEGRATING WITH OTHER TECHNOLOGIES   97

Page Decoration and Layout   98
Business Services / Dependency Injection   100
Databases   103
Security   104
Ajax   107

ABOUT THE AUTHOR   109

END NOTES   111

1

Introduction

Developing web application in Java has come a long way since the first servlet specification was released in 1997. Along the way we have learned a lot and, more than a few times, we've improved the ways we develop web applications. Apache Struts was one of those times that we made a significant stride beyond what was currently available.

Apache Struts was launched in May 2000 by Craig McClanahan, with version 1.0 officially released in July 2001. Technically it was an evolutionary step forward in web development but, more importantly, it came at the right time. Web development had been around long enough for many large projects to be built and enter maintenance phases, and for lessons to have been learned about re-usability and maintenance. Adding to this heightened need for a better solution for web application development was the "dot com boom" – as Apache Struts came on the scene in 2000, the number of web projects was dramatically increasing and it looked like there was no end in sight. The project was a welcome solution and become the de facto standard for web development for several years.

Struts2[i] is the next generation of Apache Struts. The original proposal, Struts Ti, was born out of a need to evolve Struts in a direction that the code base did not easily lend itself to. Around the time of that proposal, there was a movement by Patrick Lightbody to bring together leaders on several different web frameworks with the goal of achieving a common framework. Although the movement lost momentum, a commonality between WebWork and the goals of Struts Ti at the technology and committer level was found, and the projects were merged with WebWork providing the base technology[ii].

When we speak about WebWork we are really referencing two projects – XWork and WebWork. XWork is a generic command framework. It provides many of the core features such as actions, validation and interceptors, and is completely execution context independent. XWork also provides an internal dependency inject mechanism that is used for configuration and factory implementation management.

WebWork, on the other hand, is a completely context dependent. It provides a wrapper around XWork with the context that is needed when working on web applications, along with specific implementations that make web developer easier.

The goal of Struts2 is simple – to make web development easier for the developer. To achieve this goal Struts2 provides features to reduce XML configuration via intelligent defaults, utilizes annotations and provides conventions over configuration. Actions are now POJOs which increases testability and reduces coupling in the framework, and HTML form field data is converted to proper types for the action to use. Still further decreasing coupling is request processing has been made more modular by allowing a series of interceptors (custom or Struts2 provided) to provide pre-processing and post-processing functionality. Modularity is a common theme – a plug-in mechanism provides a way to augment the framework; key classes with the framework can be replaced with custom implementations to provide advanced features not provided out of the box; tags can utilize a variety of different rendering themes (including custom themes); and there are many different result types available for performing after-action execution tasks which include, but are not limited to, rendering JSPs, Velocity and Freemarker templates. And finally, dependency injection is now a first class citizen – provided via the Spring Framework plug-in with an option for using Plexus, and work underway for PicoContainer.

My goal with this book is to familiarize you with the Struts2 framework and provide you with a solid understanding of the components that make up the framework and the configuration options that are available. I will also introduce some ways to increase your productivity – including default configurations and implementation features to be aware of; different configuration options that are available; and development techniques. We will wrap-up with a discussion of various 3rd party integrations.

This is not a comprehensive guide to all the features of Struts2. Being a new project, Struts2 is constantly evolving with ongoing changes, updates and new features. I urge you to take some time and visit the projects home page to discover options and features not covered in this book.

This book refers to Struts2 version 2.0.6.

2

Where Struts2 fits into the Web Paradigm

There are many different web frameworks available for today's developer. Some of these come from Open Source communities, some from commercial companies, and yet others are internally developed for the current web development needs. There are over 40[iii] open source frameworks alone and, although this is a large number, there are probably as many again (if not significantly more) internally built frameworks deployed in production environments.

With so many choices out there, why choose Struts2? Here are some of the features that may lead you to consider Struts2:

- Action based framework
- Mature with a vibrant developer and user community
- Annotation and XML configuration options
- POJO-based actions that are easy to test
- Spring, SiteMesh and Tiles integration
- OGNL expression language integration
- Themes based tag libraries and Ajax tags
- Multiple view options (JSP, Freemarker, Velocity and XSLT)
- Plug-ins to extend and modify framework features

Of all the decisions in choosing a framework, choosing the style of framework is going to be the most controversial. Let's take a look at how we got to today's web application options, and where Struts2 fits into the picture.

Servlets

Servlets provided the first Java-based foray in to web development. Following the HTTP protocol, servlets provide a way to map a URL to a special class whose methods would be called.

It was quickly recognized that although this was a large step forward, generating the HTML code from within the Java code was a maintenance nightmare. Each time a simple user interface change was needed, the Java developer needed to modify the Servlet code, recompile the source and then to deploy the application into the server environment.

JSP and Scriptlet Development

As a result of this "maintenance nightmare," the style of development was turned upside-down. Rather than placing the HTML code within the Servlet or Java code, the Java code was placed (as script-lets) inside the HTML code – as Java Server Pages (JSP). Each JSP provided both the logic for processing of requests, and the presentation logic.

One problem was solved, but another was introduced. The Java code is the same as used in class files; however there is no structure of methods or classes. Looking through early JSP files, you would find one of two things:

- *Cut-and-pasted code* – Java code that has been copied from one JSP, to another, and another, etc. Propagating any defects or errors from the original code, and increasing the amount of work required to make a common change.
- *Calling common Java formatting objects* – common formatting or logic code was incorporated into a reusable object. Each JSP then used the common object.

From these findings a best practice as well as a pattern emerged – use Java objects from JSPs.

As the JSP specification evolved, tags were introduced to encapsulate re-usable java objects. Tags provided a HTML-like façade for accessing the underlying code, allowing designer (rather than developers) and IDEs to interact with dynamic elements to compose page layouts. Examples of the tags provided by JSP are `<jsp:useBean ... />` and `<jsp:getProperty ... />`. Along with the provided JSP tag libraries, JSPs provided a way for developers to create their own tag libraries.

Action-Based Frameworks

Action based frameworks came onto the scene to combine the concepts of servlets and JSPs. The idea being to split the request processing for the page the user sees into processing logic and the presentation logic, letting each part do what it does the best. The implementation used a pattern from Smalltalk known as the *model-view-controller* pattern – or more recently known as the *front controller*, or in Sun parlance *Model 2*.

In this pattern the servlet is the controller, providing a centralized point of control for all client page requests. It maps the request URL to a unit of work know as an *action*. The action's job was to perform specific functionality for a given URL by accessing the HTTP session, HTTP request and form parameter, calling business services, and then mapping the response into a *model*, whose form is a plain old java object. Finally, the action returned a result, which was mapped (via configuration files) to a JSP to render as the *view*.

Struts2 is an action based MVC web framework.

Component-Based Frameworks

As web applications became more complex, it was realized that a page was no longer the logical separation – web applications had multiple forms per page, links for content updates and many other custom widgets – all which needed processing logic to perform their tasks.

To address these complexities, component based frameworks have become popular. They provide a close tie between user interface components and classes that represent the components, and they are event-driven and more object orientated than action based frameworks. A component could be a HTML input field, a HTML form or custom widgets provided by or created for the framework. Events, such as form submits or links, are mapped to methods of the class representing the component, or to special listener classes. An additional benefit of component based frameworks is that they allow you to re-use components across multiple web applications. Examples of component based frameworks are JSF, Wicket and Tapestry.

The Great Equalizer – Ajax

In the beginning of 2005, a new fascination was starting in web development. Coined by Jesse James Garrett, Ajax stood for "Asynchronous JavaScript and XML." Relatively speaking, the technologies were nothing new. In fact, the primary web browser components for making the asynchronous calls – the `XMLHttpRequest` Object – had already been available for 6 years (since version 5 of Internet Explorer).

But what was new was the application of the technology. Google Maps was one of the first applications to take full advantage of the technology. The web page had come alive – you could interact with controls and widgets. By using a mouse you could scroll maps around the screen; when entering an address, the information would materialize above the maps images; and finally, the culmination being route planning which orchestrated all these features into a useable web application. And all of this happened without a single page refresh!

User interfaces with Ajax functionality allows the web browser to make requests to the server for smaller amounts of information, and only when it is needed. The result from the server request is formatted or manipulated and applied directly to the page being displayed, with the web browser passing on the changes to the user. Only the sections of the page that changed are re-rendered, not the entire page, making the user feel that the web application is more responsive to their actions.

The requests from the UI act like events – they are more discrete, conveying information for a single component or function. No longer does a single action need to retrieve data for the entire page, they can be more concise and thus more re-usable across applications. In effect, an Ajax user interface calling an action based framework allows the action framework to behave in a similar manner to a component based framework. In fact, this combination of technologies provides a more loosely-coupled and more re-usable system. The same actions can provide JSON, XML or HTML fragment views for the Ajax components as well as being combined with other actions to provide HTML views for non-Ajax user interfaces.

3

Core Components

From a high level, Struts2 is a pull-MVC (or MVC2) framework; this is slightly different from a traditional MVC framework in that the action takes the role of the model rather than the controller, although there is some overlap. The "pull" comes from the views ability to pull data from an action, rather than having a separate model object available.

We have already spoken about what this means conceptually, but what does it mean at the implementation level? The Model-View-Controller pattern in Struts2 is realized with five core components – actions, interceptors, value stack / OGNL, result types and results / view technologies.

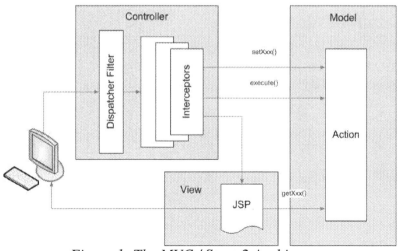

Figure 1: The MVC / Struts2 Architecture

11

Figure 1 overlays the model, view and controller to the Struts2 high level architecture. The controller is implemented with a Struts2 dispatch servlet filter as well as interceptors, the model is implemented with actions, and the view as a combination of result types and results. The value stack and OGNL provide common thread, linking and enabling integration between the other components.

As we talk about the common components in the chapter, there will be a lot of information that relates to configuration. Configuration for the web application, as well as configuration for actions, interceptors, results, etc. Keep in mind that this explanation is to provide a background for what can be achieved, and may not be the most efficient way to configure applications. In subsequent chapters we will discuss easier and more productive ways to achieve the same goal, using convention over configuration, annotations and the zero configuration plug-in.

Before we go into the details on the core components we will first talk about global configuration.

Configuration

Before configuring Struts2, you will first need to download the distribution or configure it as a dependency in your Maven2 "pom.xml" file:

```
<dependency>
    <groupId>org.apache.struts</groupId>
    <artifactId>struts2-core</artifactId>
    <version>2.0.6</version>
</dependency>
```

Maven2 is a tool for managing the entire build process of a project – including compilation of code, running tests, generating reports and managing build artifacts. The most interesting aspect for developers is in managing build artifacts.

Dependencies that your application has only need to be uniquely specified in the projects "pom.xml" configuration file using a `groupId`, `artifactId` and `version`. Before the artifact is needed, a local caching repository as well as remote organizational repositories and the standard ibiblio.com repositories are searched. If the artifact is found on a remote repository it is downloaded to the local cache and provided to the project. As well as the artifact you requested, any additional transitive dependencies that are needed by the requested artifact are also downloaded (assuming that they are in-turn specified in a "pom.xml" configuration file).

Struts2 is built with Maven2 and provides all the necessary transitive dependency configurations. For more information on Maven2, see the Apache web site at http://maven.apache.org.

Once this is done, the configuration of a Struts2 application can be broken into three separate files as shown in figure 2.

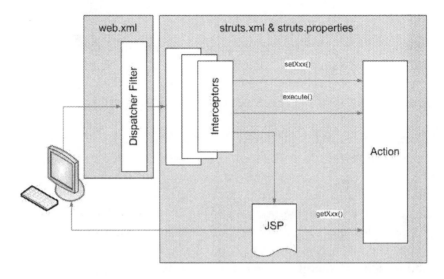

Figure 2: Configuration file scope for framework elements

The web application configuration for the `FilterDispatcher` servlet filter needs to be configured in your "web.xml" file:

```
<filter>
    <filter-name>action2</filter-name>
    <filter-class>
        org.apache.struts2.dispatcher.FilterDispatcher
    </filter-class>
</filter>

<filter-mapping>
    <filter-name>action2</filter-name>
    <url-pattern>/*</url-pattern>
</filter-mapping>
```

That's it for configuring a basic web application. What's left is to customize the web application execution environment – which is done primarily in the "struts.properties" configuration file – and to configure the components for the web application, which is achieved via the "struts.xml" configuration file. We will now look at these two configuration files in more detail.

The *struts.properties* File

This configuration file provides a mechanism to change the default behavior of the framework. Generally you will not have a need to modify this file, the exception being when you want to enable a more friendly developer debugging environment. All of the properties contained within the "struts.properties" configuration file can also be configured using the "init-param" tag in the "web.xml", as well using the "constant" tag in the "struts.xml" configuration file (we will talk about this tag's usage in the next chapter).

Properties that can be modified allow for changing Freemarker options – changing the action mapping class, determining whether XML configuration reloading should occur, what the default user interface theme is, etc. For the most up-to-date information on the properties take a looks at the Struts2 wiki at http://struts.apache.org/2.x/docs/strutsproperties.html.

A default properties file named "default.properties" is contained in the Strut2-Core JAR distribution. To enable modifications to a property, simply create a file called "struts.properties" in the root of your projects source files classpath. Then, add the properties that you wish to modify. The new values will now override the defaults.

In a development environment, there are a couple of properties that you might consider changing:
  » **struts.i18n.reload = true** – enables reloading of internationalization files
  » **struts.devMode = true** – enables development mode that provides more comprehensive debugging
  » **struts.configuration.xml.reload = true** – enables reloading of XML configuration files (for the action) when a change is made without reloading the entire web application in the servlet container
  » **struts.url.http.port = 8080** – sets the port that the server is run on (so that generated URLs are created correctly)

The *struts.xml* File

The "struts.xml" file contains the configuration information that you will be modifying as actions are developed, and we will talk in more detail about specific elements in the remaining sections in this chapter. For now, let's review the structure that won't change.

> Depending on the functionality of your application, it is possible to remove the "struts.xml" file from your application completely. The configurations that we will talk about in this chapter can be handled by alternative methods that include annotations, "web.xml" startup parameters, and alternate URL mapping schemes.
>
> The only configurations that still need the "struts.xml" file are global results, exception handling, and custom interceptor stacks.

This is an XML file, so the first element is the XML versioning and encoding information. Next is the document type definition (or DTD) for the XML. The DTD provides information on the structure the elements in the file should have, and is ultimately used by XML parsers and editor.

```
<?xml version="1.0" encoding="UTF-8" ?>
<!DOCTYPE struts PUBLIC
"-//Apache Software Foundation//DTD Struts Configuration
2.0//EN"
"http://struts.apache.org/dtds/struts-2.0.dtd">

<struts>

        <package
             name="struts2"
             extends="struts-default"
             namespace="/struts2">

             ...

        </package>

</struts>
```

We now get to the `<struts>` tag. This is the outermost tag for the Struts2 specific configuration. All other tags will be contained within this one.

The Include Tag:

The `<include ... />` tag is used to modularize a Struts2 application by including other configuration files and is always a child of the `<struts>` tag. It contains only one attribute "file" that provides the name of the file to be included – which is a file that has exactly the same structure as the "struts.xml" configuration file. For example, if you wanted to break the configuration of a billing application, you might choose to group together the billing, admin and report configurations into separate files:

```
<struts>

    <include file="billing-config.xml" />
    <include file="admin-config.xml" />
    <include file="reports-config.xml" />

    ...

</struts>
```

When including files, order is important. The information from the included file will be available from the point that the include tag is placed in the file. Hence, to use a tag that is configured in another file, the include configuration must occur before it is referenced.

As well as the files that you explicitly include, there are some that are included automatically. These are the "struts-default.xml" and the "struts-plugin.xml" files. Both contains default configurations for result types, interceptors, interceptor stacks, packages as well as configuration information for the web application execution environment (which can also configured in the "struts.properties" file). The difference is that "struts-default.xml" provides the core configuration for Struts2, where "struts-plugin.xml" provides configurations for a particular plug-in. Each plug-in JAR file should contain a "struts-plugin.xml" file, all of which are loaded during startup.

The Package Tag:

The `<package … />` tag is used to group together configurations that share common attributes such as interceptor stacks or URL namespaces. Usually this consists of action configurations, but it may include any type of configuration information. It may also be useful to organizationally separate functions, which may be further separated into different configuration files.

The attributes for this tag are:
- *name* – a developer provided unique name for this package
- *extends* – the name of a package that this package will extend; all configuration information (including action configurations) from the extended package will be available in the new package, under the new namespace
- *namespace* – the namespace provides a mapping from the URL to the package. i.e. for two different packages, with namespace attributes defined as "package1" and "package2", the URLs would be something like "/myWebApp/package1/my.action" and "/myWebApp/package2/my.action"
- *abstract* – if this attribute value is "true" the package is truly configuration grouping, and actions configured will not be accessible via the package name

It is important to make sure you are extending the correct parent package so that the necessary pre-configured features will be available to you. In most cases this will be the "struts-default" package from the "struts-default.xml" configuration file. However, when you are utilizing plug-ins it will be different. In this case, you will need to verify the needed parent package name with the plug-ins documentation.

Configuration information that belongs within the package tag will be discussed as it comes up in the remaining sections of this chapter.

There are two additional configuration elements that can be used within the `<struts>` tag. These are the `<bean ... />` and `<constant ... />` tags. These tags provide advanced ways to re-configure the framework. We will talk about the usage and configuration of these tags in the next chapter when we talk about plug-ins.

Actions

Actions are a fundamental concept in most web application frameworks, and they are the most basic unit of work that can be associated with a HTTP request coming from a user.

In Struts2 an action can be used in a couple of different ways.

Single Result

The first, and most basic usage of an action, is to perform work with a single result always being returned. In this case, the action would look like this:

```
class MyAction {

    public void String execute() throws Exception {
        return "success";
    }

}
```

A few things are worth noting. First, the action class does not need to extend another class and it does not need to implement any interfaces. As far as anyone is concerned, this class is a simple POJO.

Second, the class has one method named "execute". This name is the one used by convention. If you wanted to call it something other than "execute", the only change needed would be in the actions configuration file. Whatever the name of the method is, it will be expected to return a String result code. The actions configuration will match the result code the action returned to a specific result that will be rendered to the user. If needed, the method can also throw an exception.

The simplest configuration for the action looks like this:

```
<action name="my" class="com.fdar.infoq.MyAction" >
    <result>view.jsp</result>
</action>
```

The attribute "name" provides the URL information to execute the action, in this case a URL of "/my.action". The extension ".action" is configured in the "struts.properties"[iv] configuration file. The attribute "class" provides the full package and class name of the action to be executed.

Multiple Results

The next, slightly more complicated use is when the action can return different results depending on the outcome of the logic. The class looks similar to the previous use:

```
class MyAction {

    public void String execute() throws Exception {
        if( myLogicWorked() ) {
            return "success";
        } else {
            return "error";
        }
    }

}
```

Since there are now two different results that can be returned, we need to configure what is to be rendered back to the user for each case. Hence, the configuration will become:

```
<action name="my" class="com.fdar.infoq.MyAction" >
    <result>view.jsp</result>
    <result name="error">error.jsp</result>
</action>
```

This introduces a new "name" attribute of the result node. In fact, it has always been there. The value (as in the first result configuration) defaults to a value of "success" if not provided by the developer.

In the above sections we have seen the most common way to determine the result for an action. There are, however, four additional options available to you:

1. *The action method returns a* `String` – the `String` returned matches an action configuration in the "struts.xml" configure file. This is shown in the example.

2. *The code behind plug-in is utilized* – when the code behind plug-in is used, view templates are found by concatenating the action name with the result string returned from the action. For example, if the URL was "/adduser.action" and the action returned "success", then "/adduser-success.jsp" would be rendered. More information on the code behind plug-in can be found at http://struts.apache.org/2.x/docs/codebehind-plugin.html.

3. *The* `@Result` *annotation is used* – the action class can be annotated with a number of different results using the `@Results` and `@Result` annotations. The `String` returned from the action needs to match one of the configured annotated results.

4. *The action returns a* `Result` *class instance* – the action does not need to return a `String`, instead it can return an instance of the `Result` class that is configured and ready to use.

Result Types

The results that are generated, and returned to the user from an action for different result values, do not all need to be the same type. The result "success" may render a JSP page, but the result "error" may need to send a HTTP header back to the browser.

The type of the result (which will be discussed in more detail later in this chapter) is configured using the "type" attribute on the result node. Like the "name" attribute, there is a default value for this attribute – "dispatcher" – which will render JSPs.

Most of the time you will use provided result types, but it is possible to provide custom implementations.

Request and Form Data

In order to make decisions about how the action should work, and to provide data for database persistent objects, the action may need to access values from the request string as well as the form data.

Struts2 follows the JavaBean paradigm – if you want access to data, you provide a getter and/or setter for the field. Providing access to the request string and form values is no different. Each request string or form value is a simple name value pair, so to assign the value for a particular name, a setter is created on the action. For example, if a JSP makes a call "/home.action?framework=struts&version=2" the action would need to provide a setter "setFramework(String frameworkName)" as well as a setter "setVersion(int version)".

Notice in this example that the setter does not always need to be a String value. By default, Struts2 will convert from a String to the type on the action. This is done for all primitive types and basic object types, and can be configured for your own custom classes. Struts2 will also handle the navigation of the value into more complex object graphs, i.e. for a name on a form element name of "person.address.home.postcode" and a value of "2", Struts2 will make the equivalent call "getPerson().getAddress().getHome().setPostcode(2)".

Accessing Business Services

Up until now we have been concerned with the actions configuration, and how to control the rendering of a result back to the user for different result codes. This is an important part of what actions do but, before they return a result, some processing needs to be performed. For this, they need access to a variety of different objects – business objects, data access objects or other resources.

To provide a loosely coupled system, Struts2 uses a technique called dependency injection, or inversion of control[v]. Dependency injection can be implemented by constructor injection, interface injection and setter injection. Struts2 uses setter injection. This means that to have objects available to the action, you need only to provide a setter. The preferred dependency injection framework is the Spring Framework, which is configured via a plugin. Another option is Plexus, or if you prefer you can supply your own implementation.

There are also objects that are not managed by the spring framework, such as the `HttpServletRequest`. These are handled by using a combination of setter injection and interface injection. For each of the non-business objects there is a corresponding interface (known as an "aware" interface) that the action is required to implement.

WebWork originally had its own dependency injection framework. It was in the 2.2 release that this feature was removed and replaced by the Spring Framework. The original component framework was based on interfaces, so for each component an interface and implementation class of the interface needed to be provided.

In addition, each component had an "Aware" interface, which provided a setter for the component. If the interface was "UserDAO" the aware interface would be called "UserDAOAware" (by convention) and have one method – a setter "void setUserDAO(UserDAO dao);".

With the necessary interfaces and setters in place, interceptors will manage the injection of the necessary objects.

Accessing Data from the Action

At some point there will be a need to view objects that have been modified by the action. There are several techniques that can be used.

A familiar technique for most web developers is to place the object that needs to be accessed in the `HttpServletRequest` or the `HttpSession`. This can be achieved by implementing the "aware" interface (letting the dependency injection to do its work) and then setting the object to be accessed under the required name.

If you intend to use the built-in tag libraries or the included JSTL support, accessing the data is much easier. Both of these are able to directly access the action via the *Value Stack*. The only additional work for developers is to provide getters on the action that allows access to the objects that need to be accessed. We will talk more about the *Value Stack* in a later section.

Interceptors

Many of the features provided in the Struts2 framework are implemented using interceptors; examples include exception handling, file uploading, lifecycle callbacks and validation. Interceptors are conceptually the same as servlet filters or the JDKs `Proxy` class. They provide a way to supply pre-processing and post-processing around the action. Similar to servlet filters, interceptors can be layered and ordered. They have access to the action being executed, as well as all environmental variables and execution properties.

Let's start our discussion of interceptors with dependency injection. Injecting dependencies into the action, as we have already seen, can happen in a couple of different ways. Here are the implementing interceptors for those we have already mentioned:

- Spring Framework – the
  `ActionAutowiringInterceptor` interceptor.

- Request String and Form Values – the `ParametersInterceptor` interceptor.
- Servlet-based objects – the `ServletConfigInterceptor` interceptor.

The first two interceptors work independently, with no requirements from the action, but the last interceptor is different. It works with the assistance of the following interfaces:

- `SessionAware` – to provide access to all the session attributes via a Map
- `ServletRequestAware` – to provide access to the `HttpServletRequest` object
- `RequestAware` – to provide access to all the request attributes via a Map
- `ApplicationAware` – to provide access to all the application attributes via a Map
- `ServletResponseAware` – to provide access to the `HttpServletResponse` object
- `ParameterAware` – to provide access to all the request string and form values attributes via a Map
- `PrincipalAware` – to provide access to the `PrincipleProxy` object; this object implements the principle and role methods of the `HttpServletRequest` object in implementation, but by providing a proxy, allows for implementation independence in the action
- `ServletContextAware` – to provide access to the `ServletContext` object

For the correct data to be injected into an action, it will need to implement the necessary interface.

Configuration

If we want to enable dependency injection (or any other type of functionality provided by an interceptor) on our action we need to provide configuration. Like other elements, many interceptors have been preconfigured for you. Just make sure that the package your actions are in extends the "struts-default" package.

To configure a new interceptor, we first need to define the interceptor. The `<interceptors ... />` and `<interceptor ... />` tags are placed directly under the `<package>` tag. For the above mentioned Spring Framework interceptor, the configuration is as follows:

```
<interceptors>
    ...
    <interceptor name="autowiring"
        class="interceptor.ActionAutowiringInterceptor"/>
</interceptors>
```

We also need to ensure that the interceptor is applied to the action that requires it. This can be achieved in two ways. The first is to assign the interceptor to each action individually:

```
<action name="my" class="com.fdar.infoq.MyAction" >
    <result>view.jsp</result>
    <interceptor-ref name="autowiring"/>
</action>
```

Using this configuration there is no limitation on the number of interceptors you can apply to an action. What is required, is that the interceptors are listed in the order that they are to be executed.

The second way is to assign a default interceptor for the current package:

```
<default-interceptor-ref name="autowiring"/>
```

This declaration is made directly under the `<package ... />` tag, and only one interceptor can be assigned as the default.

Now that the interceptor has been configured for a particular action mapping, it will be executed on each and every request to the mapped URL. But this is very limiting, as most of the time we require more than one interceptor to be assigned to an action.

In fact, as Struts2 bases much of its functionality on interceptors, it is not unlikely to have 7 or 8 interceptors assigned per action. As you can imagine, having to configure every interceptor for each action would quickly become extremely unmanageable. For this reason, interceptors are managed with interceptor stacks. Here is an example, directly from the struts-default.xml file:

```
<interceptor-stack name="basicStack">
    <interceptor-ref name="exception"/>
    <interceptor-ref name="servlet-config"/>
    <interceptor-ref name="prepare"/>
    <interceptor-ref name="checkbox"/>
    <interceptor-ref name="params"/>
    <interceptor-ref name="conversionError"/>
</interceptor-stack>
```

This configuration node is placed under the `<package … />` node. Each `<interceptor-ref … />` tag references either an interceptor or an interceptor stack that has been configured before the current interceptor stack.

We have already seen how to apply interceptor to the action, applying interceptor stacks is no different. In fact, we use exactly the same tag:

```
<action name="my" class="com.fdar.infoq.MyAction" >
    <result>view.jsp</result>
    <interceptor-ref name="basicStack"/>
</action>
```

The same holds true for the configuration of the default interceptor – simply use an interceptor stack configuration name rather than an individual interceptor name.

```
<default-interceptor-ref name="basicStack"/>
```

It is therefore very important to ensure that the name is unique across all interceptor and interceptor stack configurations when configuring the initial interceptors and interceptor stacks.

Implementing Interceptors

Using custom interceptors in your application is an elegant way to provide cross-cutting application features. The interface that needs implementing is simple, and comes from the XWork framework. It has only 3 methods:

```
public interface Interceptor extends Serializable {

    void destroy();

    void init();

    String intercept(ActionInvocation invocation)
        throws Exception;
}
```

In fact, if there is no initialization or cleanup required, there is an `AbstractInterceptor` class that can be extended instead. This class provides a default no-op implementation of both the "destroy" and "init" methods.

The `ActionInvocation` object provides access to the runtime environment. It allows access to the action itself; the context (which for a web application includes the request parameters, session parameters, the users locale, etc.); the result of the actions execution; and methods to invoke the action and determine whether the action has already been invoked.

We have already seen how to configure interceptors, and configuring custom interceptors is exactly the same. If you do create your own interceptors, you will also want to consider creating custom interceptor stacks. In this manner you will ensure consistent application of the new interceptor across all actions that require it.

Value Stack / OGNL

This section covers two ideas that are closely related. The value stack is exactly what it says it is – a stack of objects. OGNL stands for Object Graph Navigational Language, and provides the unified way to access objects within the value stack.

The value stack consists of the following objects in the provided order:

1. *Temporary Objects* – during execution temporary objects are created and placed onto the value stack; an example of this would be the current iteration value for a collection being looped over in a JSP tag
2. *The Model Object* – if model objects are being used, the current model object is placed before the action on the value stack
3. *The Action Object* – the action being executed
4. *Named Objects* – these objects include `#application`, `#session`, `#request`, `#attr` and `#parameters` and refer to the corresponding servlet scopes

Accessing the value stack can be achieved in many different ways. The most common way is via the tags provided for JSP, Velocity and Freemarker. HTML tags are commonly used to access properties of objects from the value stack; control tags (such as if, elseif and iterator) are used with expressions; and data tags are available to manipulate the stack itself (via set and push).

When using the value stack there is no need to keep track of which scope the target object is in. If you want the attribute "name", then you query the value stack for this attribute. Each stack element, in the provided order, is asked whether it has the property. If it does, then the value is returned and we are done. If not, then the next element down is queried. This continues until the end of the stack is reached. This is a great feature, as you don't care where the value is – the action, the model, or the HTTP request – you just know that if the value exists it will be returned.

There is a downside. If the property is common (for example "id") and you want the value from a specific object (say the action) that is not the first object encountered with this property on the value stack, the value returned may not be what you expect. What will be returned is an "id" value, but it may be from a JSP tag, interim object, or a value from the model object. OGNL is more than just a means to access the properties of objects, and we can use this to our advantage here. If we know the depth in the stack of the action, we could use "[2].id" instead of an expression of "id",

In fact, OGNL is a fully featured expression language. As well as using dot notation to navigate object graphs (i.e. using "person.address" instead of "getPerson().getAddress()" as the expression), OGNL supports features such as type conversion, calling methods, collection manipulation and generation, projection across collections, expression evaluation and lambda expressions . The complete language guide can be found at http://www.ognl.org/2.6.9/Documentation/html/LanguageGuide/index.html.

Result Types

So far we have shown action configurations that result in a JSP being rendered to the user. This is one case, but not the only one. In fact, Struts2 supports many types of results. These can be visual, or they can be interactions with the environment.

To configure an action to execute a result of a specific type, the "type" attribute is used. If the attribute is not supplied, the default type "dispatcher" is used – this will render a JSP result. Here's what the action configuration looks like:

```
<action name="my" class="com.fdar.infoq.MyAction" >
    <result type="dispatcher">view.jsp</result>
</action>
```

Configuration

Result types are configured within the <package ... /> tag. The configuration is similar to interceptor configuration. A "name" attribute provides a unique identifier for the result type, and the "class" attribute provides the implementation class. There is a third attribute "default" – this allows the default result type to be modified. If a web application was to be based on Velocity rather than JSP, modifying the default would save time when entering configuration information.

```
<result-types>
    <result-type name="dispatcher" default="true"
        class="….dispatcher.ServletDispatcherResult"/>
    <result-type name="redirect"
        class="….dispatcher.ServletRedirectResult"/>
    …
</result-types>
```

Implementing Result Types

Similar to interceptors, it is possible to create your own result types and configure them in your web application. Many common result types already exist so, before creating your own, you should check to see if the type you want already exists.

To create a new result type, implement the `Result` interface.

```
public interface Result extends Serializable {

    public void execute(ActionInvocation invocation)
        throws Exception;
}
```

The `ActionInvocation` object provides access to the runtime environment, allowing the new result type to access information from the action that was just executed, as well as the context in which the action was executed. The context includes the `HttpServletRequest` object, which provides access to the output stream for the current request.

Results / View Technologies

In all the examples given so far, there has been an assumption that Java Server Pages (JSPs) are being rendered as the view technology. Although it may be the most common, it is not the only way to render results.

The result type is closely linked to the view technology used. In the previous section, we saw that if the "type" attribute is absent or if the value is "dispatcher", then the JSPs are rendered. There are three other technologies that can replace JSPs in a Struts2 application:

- Velocity Templates
- Freemarker Templates
- XSLT Transformations

Remember, too, that you can implement a new result type for any view technology that exists. Then you will have additional results available.

Apart from individual language syntax differences, Freemarker and Velocity are very similar to JSP. All the properties of the action (via the getter methods) are available to the template, as well as the JSP tag libraries and the use of OGNL within the tag libraries. The name of the JSP template is simply replaced with the name of either the Velocity or Freemarker template in the actions configuration. This is how a Freemarker result would be configured to be returned instead of a JSP:

```
<action name="my" class="com.fdar.infoq.MyAction" >
    <result type="freemarker">view.ftl</result>
</action>
```

The XSLT result is a little different. Instead of replacing the template name with the stylesheet name, additional parameters are used. The parameter "stylesheetLocation" provides the name of the stylesheet to use in rendering the XML. If this parameter is not present, the untransformed XML will be returned to the user.

The "exposedValue" property provides the property of the action, or an OGNL expression to be exposed as XML. If this parameter is not specified, the action itself will be exposed as XML.

```
<result type="xslt">
  <param name="stylesheetLocation">render.xslt</param>
  <param name="exposedValue">model.address</param>
</result>
```

There is also a "struts.properties" configuration property that is available when using XSLT as the result. The name of the property is "struts.xslt.nocache" and it determines whether the stylesheet is cached. During development you would want to remove any caching to allow for faster development cycles, however, when the application is deployed into production a cached stylesheet will increase performance during rendering.

Tag Libraries

Tag libraries are generally used to define a feature exclusive to JSPs that provide reusability. Freemarker and Velocity don't have the same concept; instead they provide a model or context to the rendering engine and the template being rendered has access to all those objects. When we speak of tag libraries in the Struts2 world, we are talking about objects that provide the same functionality as JSP tag libraries that are accessible to all view technologies – JSP, Velocity and Freemarker.

There is more formality around defining the tag libraries, but the underlying functionality is the same – to provide access to methods on objects. This improves maintainability by keeping the logic encapsulated, and reducing the temptation of cutting and pasting code.

JSP tag libraries have another characteristic that seems outdated in today's web development environment – to place the text to be rendered inside the Java code of the tag library itself. Struts2 has turned this idea around, creating a secondary MVC pattern exclusively for tags. Logic is provided inside Java classes, but the rendering is placed in Freemarker templates (this is a default). The entire architecture looks like this:

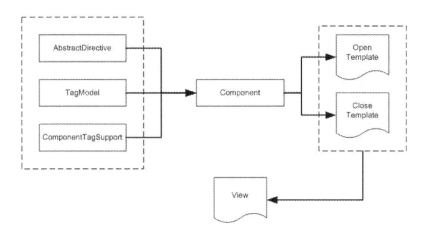

The core of the architecture is a set of component objects. The component object represents each tag in its most basic form, and provides any necessary logic as well as managing and rendering the templates. Each different result / view technology then provides a wrapper around the component. The wrapper provides the translation of what the specific view technology requires in order to use the tag within the original page.

When using the tag libraries with Freemarker template rendering, there is an additional configuration requirement. An additional servlet needs to be configured in the "web.xml" file so that Freemarker can obtain the information it needs for rendering:

```
<servlet>
   <servlet-name>jspSupportServlet</serlet-name>
   <servlet-class>
      ....action2.views.JspSupportServlet.JspSupportServlet
   </servlet-class>
   <load-on-startup>10</load-on-startup>
</servlet>
```

Each component also has templates associated with it. If the original tag contains other tags (i.e. a form tag), there will be an opening template and a closing template. If the original tag is self contained (i.e. a checkbox tag), there will be only a closing template. As well as providing a separation between text and logic within the UI architecture, using templates for tags provides an additional benefit – it allows the developer to mix and match different templates for the same tag, using a feature called "themes".

There are currently three themes[vi]: "simple", "xhtml" and "css_xhtml." The "simple" theme provides the tag output without any formatting. The "xhtml" theme takes formatting a step further; for HTML form tags, this theme provides two-column formatting using HTML tables. For CSS purists, there is the "css_chtml" theme. Similar to the "xhtml" theme this theme also provides formatting; however instead of using HTML tables it uses a CSS DIV. The additional formatting is provided to the developer without the additional clutter of HTML.

The "xhtml" and "css_xhtml" themes are good examples of what developers can do for themselves – implement a theme to provide specific formatting for HTML. Themes can be mixed and matched on the same page, and the theme for the current tag is defined using the "theme" attribute. If you are consistently using one theme, it can be set as the default using the "struts.ui.theme" property of the "struts.properties" configuration file.

Themes are provided for all tag categories (control tags, data tags, form tags and non-form UI tags); however, creating new themes is only beneficial for the visual form tags.

4

Architectural Goals

For a particular code base, the architectural goals can be difficult to determine. There are the goals that were documented before development starts; these are idealistic, and as development starts, the code usually evolves in a different direction. Then there are the true characteristics of the code base; these are harder to find, can be inconsistent across different packages or features, and are a product of evolution rather than planning.

In this chapter we will talk about five such characteristics of the Struts2 code base. Architectural elements that are still present after the evolution of the code base since 2002 – from the original WebWork, through the splitting of WebWork into WebWork2 and XWork, and the final transition into Struts2.

Separation of Concerns

As a web application developer, there are many levels of functionality that need to be addressed:

- There is the specific per-action logic that is the core of what needs to be achieved during the request/response cycle
- There is accessing or obtaining the business objects that are needed to perform the action's logic and access resources
- There is translation, mapping and conversions that need to occur in order to take a string-based value in the HTML into primitives or types and to convert view objects to business objects or database table representations

- There are cross-cutting concerns that provide functionality for groups of action, or for all actions in the application.

Within the architecture of Struts2, each of these concerns is separate. Functionality and logic no longer needs to be placed exclusively within the action. Let's take a look at of the concerns mentioned above and see how they are handled:

- *Per-Action Logic* – this is the simplest concern; each action is responsible for the logic or functionality it needs to provide
- *Accessing/Obtaining Business Objects* – Struts2 takes advantage of dependency injection, and hence the objects that are required to complete the logic in the action are supplied to the action
- *Translation/Mapping/Conversions* – each of these are slightly different concerns, but they share the common trait of being ancillary to the core actions logic. Translation and conversion of types is handled by the framework itself. String values from HTML are converted to base types and injected into the action before processing of the action starts – everything needed is already there. Mapping is handled by a specific interceptor. By configuring an action in a way that determines it to have a domain model, and specifying the fields in the HTML correctly, the framework will map the UI to the domain model. It will even traverse into an object graph.
- *Cross-cutting Concerns* – interceptors are the main feature for providing for cross-cutting functionality. Developers can implement interceptors, and then apply them across all actions, across all actions in a specific package, or pick and choose which actions that they are applied to. Another cross-cutting concern is the user interface layout. Struts2 can also help here with a feature of the supplied tags called "themes". Different themes can be developed to provide different layout options, and

then applied to individual tags, or for the entire application (by assigning it as the default).

Loose Coupling

One of the early goals of WebWork was to provide a loosely coupled framework. The 2.0 release of WebWork reinforced this, splitting the code into two projects: XWork – a generic command framework; and WebWork – the web-specific interface to XWork. This fundamental change in the architecture of WebWork created a symbiotic relationship. What was once known as "WebWork" is now essentially a combination of WebWork and XWork.

XWork, being an independent project, could now be utilized as a part of other projects – and it was. Swingwork[vii] was one such project. It was a Swing-based MVC framework that used XWork under the covers. Another example would be a JMS front end, executing or sharing XWork actions with a web UI. These provide great examples of a very high level loose coupling. Struts2 is yet another consumer of XWork.

The ideology of loose coupling is taken much further, having been integrated throughout the framework – from the very first step in processing an action to the very last. In fact, there is very little in Struts2 that cannot be configured – I believe this to be one of Struts2's greatest strengths, as well as one of its greatest weaknesses.

Common examples of loosely coupled configuration include:
- Mapping URLs to actions
- Mapping different outcomes of an action to pages that are rendered
- Mapping exceptions that occur during processing to an exception page being rendered

Less common and Struts2 specific example include:

- Configuring the business object factory if you don't want to use Spring
- Changing the way the URL is mapped to an action class
- Adding new result types for action outcomes
- Adding plug-ins for new framework functionality
- Configuring the framework level functionality via interceptors

The benefit of loosely coupled systems is well known and understood – increasing testability, extending framework features is easier, etc. But there is a downside. Because of the level of configurability, especially with respect to interceptors, the processing path of a specific action may not be understood by developers. This becomes apparent when debugging. An uninformed developer will not be able to debug quickly or efficiently due to not understanding what is happening. This problem could be as simple as an incorrectly configured interceptor, or even the order of interceptors causing issues. By understanding each piece in the processing path, solutions will come more quickly.

Testability

Unit testing has become a de facto standard in software development over the last few years. Not only does testing ensure consistency in the logic of classes but, by implementing the unit tests during (or even better, before) the development of the class under test, a less complicated and more robust design will emerge.

The predecessor of Struts2, WebWork, was built in such an environment. With loose coupling of the framework elements, testing becomes easy. The actions, interceptors, results, object factories, and other components that are developed in web application development, can be tested independently of the framework.

As actions and interceptors are the most common, we'll take a closer look at these.

Actions

Actions are invoked within the framework by convention by calling the "execute()" method, or by configuration by calling any method that returns a `String` value. From a testability standpoint, this couldn't be much easier.

Let's take a look at an example. Here is an action class that increments a number:

```
public class MyAction {

    private int number;
    public int getnumber() { return number; }
    public void setNumber( int n ) { number = n; }

    public String execute() {
        number += 10;
        return "success";
    }
}
```

As the actions are POJOs unit tests need only to instantiate the action, call the method, and then assert that the result is that which is expected. All data and resources are provided to the action via setter methods. Therefore, any data the action may need can be directly set on the action.

In our example we need two assertions – one for the outcome of the "execute" method, and the other to verify that the state of the action is what we are expecting. The unit test would then be:

```
public class myActionTest extends TestCase {

    ...

    public void testExecute() {

        MyAction action = new MyAction();
        Action.setNumber(5);
```

```
        assertEquals("success", action.execute());
        assertEquals(15,action.getNumber());
    }
}
```

Resources are only slightly more complex. Libraries such as jMock[viii] can be used to provide mock implementations of the resources, testing that interactions between the action and the resource are correct.

Although the example was written using JUnit, TestNG or any other framework could have been used.

Interceptors

When you are building interceptors, testing will be slightly more complex. However, there is additional help available. There are two scenarios when working with interceptors.

The first is when you have an interceptor that, when called, interacts with the `ActionInvocation` object. After execution, you are able to verify the logic by asserting the state of the interceptor itself. For this scenario you can test the interceptor in exactly the same way as actions. Instantiate the interceptor; create a mock implementation of the `ActionInvocation` object with values that will be used in testing the interceptor; call the `intercept` method; then assert that the changes are what is expected. These could be on the interceptor itself, the result from the method being called, or an exception that may have been thrown.

The second scenario is when the interceptor interacts with its environment or other interceptors in the interceptor stack. In this case, the test will need to interact with the action via the `ActionProxy` class, and assertions will need to access other environmental objects that the interceptor, by itself, does not have access to.

The XWork library helps here by providing the `XWorkTestCase` for JUnit tests, and the `TestNGStrutsTestCase` and `TestNGXWorkTestCase` classes for TestNG tests. These provide a test implementation for the `ConfigurationManager`, `Configuration`, `Container` and `ActionProxyFactory` class instances. Several other classes are involved, including `XWorkTestCaseHelper` and `MockConfiguration`.

Now that we have the infrastructure of setting up the environment, the test itself becomes easy - following the same steps outlined in the first scenario. The only difference being that, instead of calling the `intercept()` method on the interceptor, the execute method of the `ActionProxy` needs to be called. The following code will do this:

```
ActionProxy proxy =
    actionProxyFactory.createActionProxy(NAMESPACE,NAME,null);

assertEquals("success", proxy.execute());
```

In this scenario, tests will be asserting an expected value of the action result, values of the action, or values from the value stack. The action being executed can be obtained before or after execution by the call with:

```
MyAction action=(MyAction)proxy.getInvocation().getAction();
```

The value stack can be obtained with:

```
proxy.getInvocation().getStack()
```

Modularization

Being able to split web applications into modules becomes important as applications become large. It allows functionality or new framework features developed on one project to be packaged independently, and then re-used across other projects. Struts2 has adopted modularization as a fundamental part of the architecture, allowing developers to work independently and build upon each other's work.

There are a few ways that applications can be modularized:

- *Configuration information can be split into multiple files* – this does not affect the packaging of the application, but makes the development easier as configuration information is easier to find and logically separated along functional boundaries
- *Self-contained application modules can be created as plug-ins* – everything that is needed to provide a particular feature can be packaged together and independently distributed as a plug-in; this includes actions, interceptors, interceptor stacks, view templates (except JSPs), etc. An example is the config browser plug-in[ix], this plug-in provides a complete module that, when added to your application, provides a web interface to view configuration information
- *New framework feature plug-ins can be created* – new functionality that is non-application specific can be bundled as a plug-in and used across many difference applications

Technically speaking, all of these ways to modularize an application are the same – they have the same configuration elements (except the name might be different; "struts-plugin.xml" is the configuration file that is automatically loaded for plug-ins), the same directory structure, and they can contain the same framework and application elements.

The only difference between the two types of plug-ins is how you conceptually think of them, and which elements and configurations are put in the distribution package.

Additional Configuration Elements

Because plug-ins can provide alternate implementations for internal framework functionality, there are additional configuration elements. Although these elements can be used in the "struts.xml" configuration file, and are used in the "struts-default.xml" file, they are used more common in configuring plug-ins.

For plug-ins, configuration of alternate implementations happens in two steps:

1. The alternate interface implementation is provided using the `<bean ... />` tag, along with a unique key that identifies it
2. One of possibly many configured interface implementations is selected using the `<constant ... />` tag

Let's take a look at each of these steps in more detail.

The `<bean ... />` tag allows plug-ins to supply implementation information for extension points. Below is an example that shows the configuration of an object factory from the "struts-default.xml" configuration file:

```
<bean name="struts"
  type="com.opensymphony.xwork2.ObjectFactory"
  class="org.apache.struts2.impl.StrutsObjectFactory" />
```

Attributes provide everything that is needed to create and utilize an alternate object implementation within Struts2. The attributes that can be used are:

- *class* – this provides the full name of the class
- *type* – this is the interface the class implements
- *name* – a short name that is unique per *type*

- *static* – whether to inject static class methods into the class instance
- *scope* – the scope that an instance is utilized in, this can be "default", "request", "session", "singleton" or "thread"
- *optional* – if "true" loading will continue even if there was an error creating an instance of the class

Next, the `<constant ... />` tag allows the developer to select which configuration is used. There are only two attributes – a property name that provides the name of the extension point that your new implementation is changing, and the value which is the unique name configured using a `<bean ... />` tag.

```
<constant name="struts.objectFactory" value="plexus" />
```

The `<constant ... />` tag is one way to apply a new value to a known property, but it is not the only way. The value can also be modified using an "init-param" in the "web.xml" configuration file, or as a name-value pair in the "struts.properties" configuration file.

If you are not developing a plug-in, but instead using these techniques in a regular "struts.xml" configuration file, there is a shortcut. In the `<constant ... />` tag, use the class value that you would normally place in the `<bean ... />` tag – this avoids the need for the `<bean ... />` tag altogether.

This table lists the interfaces and the property names for the configurable extension points.

Interface	Property Name	Scope	Description
com.opensymphony. xwork2. ObjectFactory	struts.object Factory	singleton	Creates objects used in the framework - actions, results, interceptors, business, objects.

com.opensymphony. xwork2. ActionProxyFactory	struts. actionProxyFactory	singleton	Creates the ActionProxy
com.opensymphony. xwork2.util. ObjectType Determiner	struts. objectTypeDeterminer	singleton	Determines what the key and the element class of a map or collection are
org.apache.struts2. dispatcher.mapper. ActionMapper	struts.mapper.class	singleton	Determines the ActionMapping from a request and a URI from an Action Mapping
org.apache.struts2. dispatcher.multipart. MultiPartRequest	struts.multipart. parser	per request	Parses a multipart Request (file upload)
org.apache.struts2. views.freemarker. FreemarkerManager	struts.freemarker. manager.classname	singleton	Loads and processes Freemarker templates
org.apache.struts2. views.velocity. VelocityManager	struts.velocity. manager.classname	singleton	Loads and processes Velocity templates

The `<constant … />` tag and "init-param" in the "web.xml" configuration file is not limited to only extension point properties. Any property from the "struts.properties" configuration file can be modified using the same technique.

Convention over Configuration

Convention over configuration is a concept that Rails has brought to main stream application development. Rather than providing configuration files, which were very similar between applications, an assumption was made that under *most* circumstances developers would follow a particular pattern. The pattern being followed was considered generic enough to be deemed a convention and, rather than having to provide the configuration for each new application, it was provided by the framework as the default. As the default, developers no longer needed to provide the configuration information. However, if there was a need to deviate from the convention configuration information, it could be provided to override the defaults.

Struts2 has adopted this concept. Loose coupling has provided an opportunity for Struts2 to be extremely flexible, but it also means that the framework can be extremely difficult to configure. Conventions balance out these two opposing forces, allowing for a simpler and more productive developer experience.

Examples of convention over configuration in Struts2 include:

- *Implicit Configuration File Loading* – rather than explicitly configuring the "struts-default.xml" file and "struts-plugin.xml" file (for each plug-in), they are loaded automatically during startup
- *Code Behind Plug-in* – when utilizing the code behind plug-in, the result template is automatically searched for using a combination of the action name and result string, so that for an action "/user/add.action" the result template "/user/add-success.jsp" will be returned for a "success" result, and the result template "/user/add-error.jsp" would be returned for an "error" result
- *Default Result & Result Type* – when configuring actions there is no need to specify the result and the type when using the default of "success" and JSP
- *Wiring of Spring Business Service* – with the Spring framework plug-in installed, it is not necessary to configure each Spring-provide business service that each action requires; instead, the business service is wired into the action automatically

In previous chapters we have seen several default settings, as well as how to override the values and provide new defaults via configuration. More configuration options, as well as more conventions will be explored in the upcoming chapter on productivity features.

5

Productivity Tips

This chapter contains a list of tips, techniques, features and things to keep in mind to be as productive as possible when developing web applications using Struts2. Some tips may be as simple as listing default values, and some as complex as showing the interface that needs to be implemented to create custom declarative validations.

The information provided in this section is intended only as an introduction – if a tip looks interesting, dig a little deeper. Go to the Struts2 documentation at http://struts.apache.org/2.x/docs/guides.html or do a search to see what other developers think and how they have used it.

Finally, as you read each section think about how this tip may interact with other tips; think about how this tip may be different from other tips; and think about how you can utilize the tip in your web development. Take your understanding to the next level.

Having a plug-in architecture allows Struts2 to continuously evolve. Regular visits to the Struts2 plug-in registry page will keep you up to date on the latest developments. This page is the source for all plug-in related announcements, and it can be found at http://cwiki.apache.org/S2PLUGINS/home.html. It already contains several 3rd party plug-ins for JSON, GWT and Spring WebFlow functionality.

Re-Using Action Configurations

We have talked about configuring actions into packages, and about how packages can extend other packages - but the benefit of this may not be clear. Let's take a look at a concrete example. The example is an application that provides information to visitors of zoos. There will be a portal page for each continent providing information including animals, maps, etc.

One way to handle this feature request is to provide one action that the user can invoke with a URL something like "www.myzoo.com/home.action?continent=asia". This consolidates the application logic and makes it easy to determine which continent is being requested. However, depending on how the information to be rendered to the user is defined, flexibility could be lost as hard coded path information is added to the action or view.

A more flexible solution is to provide a URL such as "www.myzoo.com/asia/home.action". Using this scheme, a base action would be provided and configured in the default package. Each inheriting package then has access to the same action. So "www.myzoo.com/home.action" calls exactly the same class as "www.myzoo.com/asia/home.action" – without any additional configuration.

Furthermore, the views can also be also customized without any additional configuration. If the configuration of the action (in the default package) is

```
<action name="home" class="com.fdar.infoq.HomeAction" >
    <result>portal.jsp</result>
</action>
```

then the JSP that is rendered by Struts2 will depend on the users calling namespace, as provided by the URL. Hence, if the URL is "www.myzoo.com/home.action" the "/portal.jsp" will be rendered, but if the URL is "www.myzoo.com/asia/home.action" is called, the JSP "/asia/portal.jsp" will be rendered. Once again, this functionality is provided without any additional configuration – because the configuration provides a relative JSP location rather than a specific one.

Use Pattern Matching Wildcards in Configurations

Action configuration files are somehow able to grow to extremely large at incredible speeds. On way to combat this phenomenon is to use pattern matching. Pattern matching works by defining one or more patterns that URLs will conform to.

An example will be an easy way to see how things work. Let's say that the URLs in your web application always follows the pattern "/{module}/{entity}/{action}.action". This is a common pattern; examples would be the URL's "/admin/User/edit.action", "/admin/User/list.action" and "/admin/User/add.action".

The class configuration is such that there is a Struts2 action class with the name "{entity}Action", and each {action} is method on the action class. All the results from invoking the action's methods will result in either the update page for the entity being displayed, or a list of all the entities being displayed.

For our example, the "struts.xml" configuration will look like this:

```
<action name="*/*/*" method="{3}"
        class="com.infoq.actions.{1}.{2}Action">
    <result name="view">/{1}/update{2}.jsp</result>
    <result name="list">/{1}/list.jsp</result>
</action>
```

Each asterisk in the actions name is a wildcard. In the example, only asterisks are used – but this need not be the case. For example, say you wish to map all entity view actions together. Something like 'name="/*/View*"' would do the trick. Token identifiers, {1}, {2}, etc., are then used to obtain the text values harvested from the wildcards (where the numeric value correlating to the position of the asterisk, ascending from left to right).

In the "struts.properties" configuration file (or using the constant tag in the "struts.xml" configuration file) you need to ensure the following property is correctly set:

```
struts.enable.SlashesInActionNames = true
```

This property allows slashes in the name of the action. Struts2's default configuration is to not have slashes in the action name, instead using packages for namespace separation.

Finally, there is no shortcut if you are providing validation and conversion property files rather than using annotations. We'll talk about this more in following sections. Each needs to contain the full name of the action, along with the necessary extension: i.e. "edit-validation.xml" and "edit-conversion.xml" for the original example, in the "com.infoq.actions.admin" package.

Utilize Alternate URI Mapping Schemes

A different approach than using wildcards in the configuration, is to provide a custom mapping from the URI to the action and method being invoked. Using this technique there will be less configuration, and the mapping will be applied consistently across the entire application. You can utilize URI patterns combined with session information, or any other information you can imagine, to determine the action to be called.

The interface that needs to be implemented is the `ActionMapper`, and it has two methods to implement: the `getMapping()` method that converts a URI into a known configuration; and the `getUriFromActionMapping()` method that converts an action configuration into a URI.

```
public interface ActionMapper {

    ActionMapping getMapping(
        HttpServletRequest request,
        ConfigurationManager configManager);

    String getUriFromActionMapping(
        ActionMapping mapping);
}
```

The `ActionMapping` class provides the resulting actions namespace, name, method, result and parameters. And the `ConfigurationManager` provides access to configuration providers (which in turn allow for further customization).

To install the action mapper, the current action mapper needs to be replaced in the "struts.xml" configuration file. The name and the type are always the same - the difference is that the class value is that of the custom ActionMapper type that has been implemented.

```
<constant name="struts.mapper.class"
    value="com.fdar.infoq.MyActionMapper" />
```

The good news is that you don't need to go through the effort of implementing an ActionMapper to take advantage of this feature. Struts2 has implemented several different types.

The `Restful2ActionMapper` class provides an implementation of a ReST-style interface, and was inspired by the easy-to-use URIs of Ruby on Rails. Something to keep in mind is that this implementation is marked as experimental in the Struts2 documentation.

The first thing that the `Restful2ActionMapper` does is determine the namespace and action that is to be used. This is achieved as you would expect – the last element in the URL is the name of the action, with the values before the action becoming the namespace. The exception to this is that attributes may also be passed in the URL, with the pattern used to map the action name and the attribute name and values to the URI being:

```
http://HOST/PACKAGE/ACTION/PARAM_NAME1/PARAM_VALUE1/PARAM
_NAME2/PARAM_VALUE2
```

There is no limit to the number of "PARAM_NAME/PARAM_VALUE" pairs that you can have in the URI, and if the PARAM_NAME1 is "id" the URI can be shortened to:

```
http://HOST/PACKAGE/ACTION/PARAM_VALUE1/PARAM_NAME2/PARAM
_VALUE2
```

Once the action is known, the next step is to find the method to invoke on the action. The HTTP method is used for this determination. As HTML doesn't support PUT and DELETE methods, an additional request attribute "__http_method" provides the method information.

Here's what happens for HTTP method and URL combinations:

- GET: "/user" – when the action is used alone the "index" method is invoked
- GET: "/user/23" – when the action is used with parameter name/value pairs the "view" method is invoked, in this case the "id" attribute is set to a value of "23"
- POST: "/user/23" – when the method is POST rather than GET, the "create" method is invoked; the "id" (or other identifying values) may be contained in the URL, and the name-value pairs containing information to update will be in the POST data
- PUT: "/user" – the "update" method is invoked; similar to the POST scenario, the name-values pairs containing data will be in POST data rather than the URL
- DELTE: "/user/23" – the "remove" method is invoked, with the unique identifier (in this case the "id" attribute having a value of "23") supplied in the URL

- GET: "/user/23!edit" – the "!" is used to supply the method name to use, so in this case the "edit" method will be invoked
- GET: "/user/new" – the "new" suffix indicates that the "editNew" method is to be invoked

There is also a `CompositeActionMapper` class. This implementation allows you to chain different individual ActionMapper implementations together. Each is checked in the listed sequence to determine if it can resolve the URI. If the URI can be resolved, the result is returned. If not, the next implementation in sequence will be checked; if no match is found a null result is returned.

As well as the normal `ActionMapper` configuration, the configuration for the `CompositeActionMapper` includes a constant that lists the class names of the `ActionMapper` implementations that are to be chained together.

```
<bean name="struts"
    type="….dispatcher.mapper.ActionMapper"
    class="….dispatcher.mapper.CompositeActionMapper" />

<constant name="struts.mapper.composite"
    value="….dispatcher.mapper.DefaultActionMapper,
            ….dispatcher.mapper.RestfulActionMapper" />
```

Know Interceptor Functionality

Interceptors play a vital role in providing functionality to the Struts2 framework. By knowing the available interceptors you will understand what processing is happening during each step of the processing of an action.

Another side benefit is with debugging actions. There will be times that the action does not contain the data that is expected. In these circumstances it is more often than not a problem with either an interceptor not being applied when it should have, or interceptors being applied in an incorrect order. By understanding what each interceptor does, zeroing in on the problem and correcting it will be easy.

Here is a list of the interceptors that are provided out of the box, as well a description of the functionality that each provides.

Interceptor Name	Description
alias	Converts similar parameters that may be named differently between requests.
chain	Makes the previous Action's properties available to the current Action. Commonly used together with `<result type="chain">` (in the previous Action).
conversionError	Adds conversion errors from the ActionContext to the Action's field errors
createSession	Create an `HttpSession` automatically, useful with certain Interceptors that require a `HttpSession` to work properly (like the `TokenInterceptor`)
debugging	Provides several different debugging screens to provide insight into the data behind the page.
execAndWait	Executes the action in the background and then sends the user off to an intermediate waiting page.
exception	Maps exceptions to a result.
fileUpload	An interceptor that adds easy access to file upload support.
I18n	Remembers the locale selected for a user's session.
logger	Outputs the name of the action.
model-driven	If the Action implements ModelDriven, pushes the `getModel` Result onto the Value Stack.
scoped-model-driven	If the action implements

	`ScopedModelDriven`, the interceptor retrieves and stores the model from a scope and sets it on the action calling `setModel()`.
params	Sets the request parameters onto the Action.
static-params	Sets the "struts.xml" defined parameters onto the action. These are the `<param …` `/>` tags that are direct children of the `<action … />` tag.
scope	Simple mechanism for storing action state in the session or application scope.
servlet-config	Provide access to Maps representing `HttpServletRequest` and `HttpServletResponse`.
timer	Outputs how long the action takes to execute (including nested Interceptors and View)
token	Checks for valid token presence in action, prevents duplicate form submission.
token-session	Same as token interceptor, but stores the submitted data in session when handed an invalid token
validation	Performs validation using the validators defined in *action-validation.xml*
workflow	Calls the `validate` method in your action class. If action errors are created then it returns the `INPUT` view.
store	Store and retrieve action messages / errors / field errors for action that implements `ValidationAware` interface into session.
checkbox	Adds automatic checkbox handling code that detect an unchecked checkbox and add it as a parameter with a default (usually 'false') value. Uses a specially named hidden field to detect unsubmitted checkboxes. The default unchecked value

	is overridable for non-boolean valued checkboxes.
profiling	Activate profiling through parameter
roles	Action will only be executed if the user has the correct JAAS role.
prepare	If the action implements `Preparable`, calls it's `prepare()` method.

Use Provided Interceptor Stacks

Interceptor stacks provide functional groupings of interceptors to apply to different action categories. Stacks can be constructed for CRUD operations, for validation of action inputs or for anything else you may need. But before you start creating your own stacks, take a look at what Struts2 provides out of the box. Many standard configurations have already been constructed and are ready to use. Additionally, each plug-in can provide its own interceptor stack, which should be used if utilizing the functionality.

There are two ways to utilize the provided interceptor stacks – either place you actions in the package that provides the interceptor stack (using the zero configuration annotation or "struts.properties" constant), or have new packages that you define (that includes your action) extend the package that provides the interceptor stack:

```
<package name="mypackage"
    extends="struts-default" namespace="/mypackage">
    ...
</package>
```

Having said this, before deploying an application into production you should always take a look at the interceptor stacks being used to determine whether you need each and every interceptor. The "paramsPrepareParamsStack" and "defaultStack" contain interceptors such as "chain", "il8n", "fileUpload", "profiling" and "debugging". These are not commonly used, and by removing them you can avoid unnecessary processing work.

Stack Name	Description
basicStack	The most basic stack provided by Struts2. Provides exception handling, HTTP objects and request/form parameters are injected into the action, and conversion errors handled.
Validation WorkflowStack	Adds validation and workflow to the basic stack.
fileUploadStack	Adds automatic file uploading support to the basic stack.
modelDrivenStack	Adds support for model driven actions to the basic stack.
chainStack	Adds action chaining support to the basic stack.
i18nStack	Adds internationalization to the basic stack.
paramsPrepare ParamsStack	This is the most complex stack provided. It is used when request parameters are to be applied to an action to load data (or perform other task) when the `prepare()` method is called, and then the request parameters re-applied to override some of the loaded values. A good example of using this stack is for an object update. The id is used to load the object out of the database, and then the data from the request is used to override some of the data loaded.
defaultStack	This is the default stack. For most scenarios it provides all the functionality that is required. In fact, it includes nearly all the interceptors available in the core

	distribution.
completeStack	This stack provides backward compatibility for WebWork applications by providing an alias to the "defaultStack".
executeAnd WaitStack	Adds asynchronous execution of actions to the default stack.

Take Advantage of Result Types

Result types allow the developer to mix and match how elements are rendered back to the user of the web application. In fact, one action could have multiple results and each can be configured with different result types.

Another important thing to keep in mind when developing, is that results can be visual as well as non-visual. For example, returning HTTP headers.

Here is the list of the pre-configured result types, and a brief explanation of what they do. All of these are available when you place you action within, or extend the "struts-default" package in your application:

Name	Description
chain	Chains from the execution of one action to another configured action. Copies all property values with getter methods from the initial action to corresponding setter methods on the target action.
dispatcher	Renders Java server pages. This is the default result type, and is used if no result type is configured in the action configuration.
freemarker	Renders Freemarker templates.
httpheader	Returns HTTP headers with user defined values.

redirect	Redirects to any arbitrary URL.
redirect-action	Redirect to a configured action. Can be used to provide redirect after post functionality.
stream	Streams data back to the browser. Used to stream PDF, Microsoft Word, images, or other data.
velocity	Renders Velocity templates.
xslt	Uses an XSLT to format the properties from the action that has been previously executed.

Utilize Data Conversion

A common task for web development is converting the string based form data to the correct types for the model, or for business service methods. Usually this is a code- intensive manual process. Struts2 expedites the process by providing data conversion for you. The built in conversion will convert a `String` to any of the following:

- `String`
- `Boolean` or `boolean`
- `Character` or `char`
- `Integer` or `int`
- `Float` or `float`
- `Long` or `long`
- `Double` or `double`
- `Date` – using the locale associated with the current request

The setter provided on the action can then change from "setId(String id)" to "setId(int id)". We no longer need to do conversions for each value, and can simply use the value with the correct type that has been set on the action.

For custom type conversions you can implement the class `StrutsTypeConverter`. There are two methods that need to be implemented; one to convert from a string to a new type class, and the other to convert from the new type back to a string.

```
public class MyTypeConverter extends StrutsTypeConverter{

    public Object convertFromString(
        Map context, String[] values, Class toClass) {
        ...
    }

    public String convertToString(Map context, Object o){
        ...
    }
}
```

If there is a problem during the conversion, a `TypeConversonException` should be thrown to indicate to the framework that the conversion could not be completed.

To use the new converter in your action class you need to configure it. This can be achieved using annotation (discussed in a later section) or by using a separate "*-conversion.properties" file. If the action class that is using the conversion is called "MyAction", then you would create a file in the same package called "MyAction-conversion.properties". The file contents would be:

```
typeVal = MyTypeConverter
```

The left hand side value "typeVal" is the name of the request or form value that needs to be converted, and on the right is the full path and class name of the converter.

If you are using the conversion for multiple actions, you can avoid configuring each individually and instead use the global configuration file "xwork-conversion.properties". This file is placed in the classpath root of your application. The contents of the file would be:

```
MyType = MyTypeConverter
```

Both values need to be the full path and name of the type class and the converter class. Notice here that the class name of the type rather than the name of the request or form value is used. Hence, the setter on the action would be "setTypeValue(MyType type)".

Utilize Tabular Data Entry Support

Struts2 provides support for using lists to transfer tabulated data easily between the HTML user interface and actions. Let's take a look at an example. Here is a class for Person; each attribute has a getter and setter (not shown):

```
public class Person {
    int id;
    String name;
    int age;
    float height;
}
```

Our action would then use the person class in a list:

```
public class MyAction {

    public List getPeopleList() { … }
    public void setPeopleList( List peopleList ) { … }

    …
}
```

Before we can use the `Person` class as an element in `MyAction`, we need to add configuration information. This is achieved with the "MyAction-conversion.properties" file, which is created in the same package as `MyAction`. The name follows the same convention as for validation, the name of the action followed by a "*-conversion.properties" suffix. The file contents are:

```
Element_peopleList=Person
```

The prefix "Element_" is constant, with the last part of the left-hand value being the name of the list property in the action class.

The right-hand side value is the full class name (including package) of the class that is placed into the list.

To finish the example we need to render the list to the user:

```
<ww:iterator value="peopleList" status="stat">
   <s:property value="peopleList[#stat.index].id" />
   <s:property value="peopleList[#stat.index].name" />
   <s:property value="peopleList[#stat.index].age" />
   <s:property value="peopleList[#stat.index].height"/>
</ww:iterator>
```

Lists are indexed, so we use the index property of the iterators status object to reference the element being displayed. This is not the most efficient way of achieving this particular result, as the value of the `<s:property … />` tags could have been simply "id", "name", "age" and "height" respectively. What it does show is a clean form of what is needed for an editable form.

For a tabular editable form using the same objects, the JSP is:

```
<s:form action="update" method="post" >

    <s:iterator value="peopleList" status="stat">

        <s:hidden
            name="peopleList[%{#stat.index}].id"
            value="%{peopleList[#stat.index].id}"/>
        <s:textfield label="Name"
            name="peopleList[%{#stat.index}].name"
            value="%{peopleList[#stat.index].name}"/>
        <s:textfield label="Age"
            name="peopleList[%{#stat.index}].age"
            value="%{peopleList[#stat.index].age}" />
        <s:textfield label="Height"
            name="peopleList[%{#stat.index}].height"
            value="%{peopleList[#stat.index].height}"/>
        <br/>

    </s:iterator>

    <s:submit value="Update"/>

</s:form>
```

Notice that the "name" and "value" attribute of this code is similar to the "value" attribute above. The difference being in the "name" we need to provide the actual index by surrounding "#stat.index" with the correct token to obtain a value, and the "value" attribute has the entire expression surrounded. Using this code, Struts2 will create an `ArrayList` with populated `People` objects, and set the list on the action using the `setPeopleList()` method.

To allow Struts2 to create new objects in the list (perhaps you are dynamically creating elements in the user interface), add the following line to "MyAction-conversion.properties" configuration file:

```
CreateIfNull_peopleList = true
```

Expose Domain Models in the Action

With both data conversion and collections, we have started to introduce a trend. Rather than using `String` values for HTML form field, proper types can be used. We have also seen that request attributes and form field values are set directly on the action via property setter methods.

We can take this a step further. Struts2 introduces the notion of a "model-driven action," reducing the code that is needed to map the field from the user interface to those of domain objects or value objects that are used when calling business services.

For an action to be model-driven, it needs to implement the `ModelDriven` interface. This has one method that is to return the object that the action has designated as the model.

```
public interface ModelDriven {

    java.lang.Object getModel();
}
```

The interceptor stack that is used for processing the action also needs to contain the "model-driven" interceptor. Stacks that include this interceptor are "modelDriven", "defaultStack", "paramsPrepareParamsStack" and "completeStack". This interceptor obtains the model object from the action, and places it on the value stack ahead of the action so that request or form values are set on the model instead of the action. Similarly, in reverse, the values being used and displayed in the JSP will be obtained from the model.

This is not an "all or nothing" scenario. If there are request or form values that do not have a corresponding setter on the model, they will be passed through and be set on the action. And if the JSP doesn't find a value on the model, it will continue down the value stack to obtain the information from the action.

These techniques together allow you to set or retrieve values on either the model or action, without needing to explicitly specify the target.

Use Declarative Validation Where Possible

There are two possible ways to provide validation in the Struts2 application – programmatically and declaratively.

To provide validation programmatically, an action needs to implement the `Validateable` interface. This has one method, which should contain the validations:

```
void validate();
```

To report validation problems back to the user, your action needs to implement the `ValidationAware` interface. This is a more complex interface, providing methods to add validation errors, determine whether there are currently validation errors, etc.

If possible, your action can extend the `ActionSupport` class, which provides a default implementation for both these interfaces. Programmatic validations should only be used when the validations are extremely complex. A better solution for validation is to provide them declaratively.

Each action that requires declarative validations will need either annotations (which will be discussed in a later section) on the action class, or a corresponding XML file. For the action MyAction, the file would be named "MyAction-validation.xml", and be in the same package as the action. The interceptor stack that processes the action will also need to include the "validation" (responsible for performing the validation) and "workflow" (responsible for redirecting the user back to the "input" result if a validation failure occurred) interceptors. Stacks that contain these interceptors are the "validationWorkflowStack", paramsPrepareParamsStack , "defaultStack" and "completeStack".

Here is an example of the validation file:

```
<!DOCTYPE validators PUBLIC
"-//OpenSymphony Group//XWork Validator 1.0.2//EN"
"http://www.opensymphony.com/xwork/xwork-validator-
1.0.2.dtd">
<validators>
    <field name="count">
        <field-validator type="int" short circuit="true">
            <param name="min">1</param>
            <param name="max">100</param>
            <message key="invalid.count">
                Value must be between ${min} and${max}
            </message>
        </field-validator>
    </field>
    <field name="name">
        <field-validator type="requiredstring">
            <message>You must enter a name.</message>
        </field-validator>
    </field>
    <validator type="expression"short-circuit="true">
        <param name="expression">
            email.equals(email2)
        </param>
        <message>Email not the same as email2</message>
    </validator>
</validators>
```

A couple of things to note from this example:
- Each field can have one or more "field-validator" nodes
- Each fields validators are executed in the order they are defined
- Each field validator has a "short-circuit" attribute; if this is true and the validation fails, all further validations are skipped and a failed result returned for the field
- The message node can include a "key" attribute which looks up the message to display to the user from a message bundle; the value of the node is then used if no message bundle key exists
- Validator configuration information (such as min and max) as well as values from the value stack can be used in the validation message by placing the value between the tokens "${" and "}"
- Validators can have a scope of either "field" or "expression"; expression validators can work across multiple fields

Below is the full list of validator types along with their descriptions. More information, including configurations, can be found at http://struts.apache.org/2.x/docs/validation.html.

Name	Description
required	Ensures that the property is not null
requiredstring	Ensures that a `String` property is not null and not empty
stringlength	Checks whether a `String` is within a specific length range
int	Checks whether an `int` property is within a specific range
double	Checks whether a `double` property is within a specific range
date	Checks whether a `date` property is within a specific range
expression	Evaluates an ONGL expression (which

	must return a boolean) using the value stack
fieldexpression	Validates a field using an OGNL expression
email	Ensures the property is a valid email address
url	Ensures that the property is a valid URL
conversion	Checks whether the there was a conversion error for the property
regex	Checks whether the property value matches the regular expression
visitor	The visitor validator defers the validation of a field to another validation file specific to the class of the field. For example, you are using a model driven actions and each has a property called "person" which is a class `Person`. If this same model is used across many actions you will want to extract the validation information and re-use it. The visitor validation type allows this functionality.

In addition to those validators provided by Struts2, you can write your own. Your custom validator would need to implement the `Validator` interface (for expression validations) or the `FieldValidator` interface (for field validations).

The new validator would need to be registered in a "validators.xml" file, which is placed in the classpath root directory. Usually this file is accessed from the distribution JAR file, but when one is provided the distribution file is ignored. So if you intend to add any new validators you will need to copy it from the Struts2 JAR into the root of the classpath directory, so that all the current validators are included in your application, and then add your new validators. Like other configuration it is relatively easy, consisting of a chosen unique name and the class name of the validator.

```
<validators>
    <validator name="postcode"
        class="com.validators.PostCodeValidator"/>
    ...
</validators>
```

Move CRUD Operations into the same Action

By combining a model-driven action with the "preparable" interceptor/interface, wildcards in the action configuration, validation and workflow you can simplify CRUD operations into a single action. This approach provides similar functionality to using the Restful2ActionMapper.

The URL pattern we are using is "/{model}/{method}.action". For example, we want "/User/add.action" to call the "add" method on the UserAction class. We also need to ensure that there are several result mappings – for "success" (the default), "input" (for validation problems) and a "home" or default page. Each of these pages will be specific to the model. The "success" mapping redirects to an action, following the redirect-after-post pattern.

The "struts.xml" configuration to manage this is:

```
<action name="*/*" method="{2}"
    class="com.infoq.actions.{1}Action">
    <result type="redirect">/{1}/view.action</result>
    <result name="view">/{1}/view.jsp</result>
    <result name="input">/{1}/edit.jsp</result>
    <result name="home">/{1}/home.jsp</result>
</action>
```

The action will need to extend the ActionSupport class (providing validation and error message handling implementations) and implement the ModelDriven and

`Preparable` interfaces. The interceptor stack along with the two interfaces is the key to making the implementation easy, so let's take a look at those in more detail.

The `ModelDriven` interface provides one method, `getModel()` which, in conjunction with the "model-driven" interceptor, places the model from the action on the value stack ahead of the action. When request parameters are being set, they are applied to the model rather than the action. This is what we are after – setting the values on the model and not the action – as we can then just update the action. But what if there are data values already on the model that we do not wish to override?

This is where the "paramsPrepareParamsStack" interceptor stack comes into play. The steps that we want performed, and the interceptors within the stack that performs them are:

1. Set the id on the action – *the "params" interceptor*
2. Allow the action to perform some logic to either create a new model, or obtain an existing model from a service or the database – *the "prepare" interceptor calling the* `prepare()` *method from the* `Preparable` *interface*
3. Now that the model exists, set the request attributes onto the model – *the "model-driven" interceptor, followed by the "params" interceptor again*
4. Check the model for validation problems and redirect back to the input page if necessary – *the "validation" and "workflow" interceptors*
5. Execute the logic for the method being invoked - *normal action processing*

By following these conventions, every model or entity object in your web application can be managed with the "struts.xml" configuration above. What will change is the action implementation. Following our `User` example, this is what the `UserAction` class will look like:

```
public class UserAction
    extends ActionSupport
    implements ModelDriven, Preparable{
    private User user;
```

```
    private int id;
    private UserService service; // user business service

    ...

    public void setId(int id) {
        this.id = id;
    }

    /** create a new user if none exists, otherwise
        load the user with the specified id */
    public void prepare() throws Exception {
        if( id==0 ) {
            user = new User();
        } else {
            user = service.findUserById(id);
        }
    }

    public Object getModel() {
        return user;
    }

    /** create or update the user and then
        view the created user */
    public String update() {
        if( id==0 ) {
            service.create(user);
        } else {
            service.update(user);
        }
        return "redirect";
    }

    /** delete the user and go to a default home page */
    public String delete() {
        service.deleteById(id);
        return "home";
    }

    /** show the page allowing the user to
        view the existing data */
    public String view() {
        return "view";
    }

    /** show the page allowing the user to view
        the existing data and change the values */
    public String edit() {
        return "input";
    }
}
```

The `edit()` method is invoked by the user when they want to create a new user or edit an exiting user. This method is simple, returning "input", which returns a page with a HTML form on it. The form action target URL that is mapped to the `update()` method. The `update()` method could have been split into two separate methods, but this would complicate the HTML form and makes little sense as it is easy to determine whether the object exists by using a unique key field.

Finally, the `view()` method is a simple pass-through method, forwarding to a page that displays the user, and the `delete()` method removed the user with the specified id and returns to the user's default home page.

All of these methods have little or no logic within them, and could easily be mistaken for doing nothing. In fact, there is functionality, but it is a cross-cutting concern and as such has been refactored into the `prepare()` method. For each of the `edit()`, `update()` and `view()` methods – if there is a model that exists it needs to be retrieved, and if there is no model then one needs to be created.

The action is still relatively simple, and could be easily parameterized allowing it to be generated for different model classes and services. With this infrastructure in place, the most complex piece of developing a CRUD application is creating the page templates.

Use Annotation Where Possible

Struts2 was developed for JDK 5, and as such is able to utilize annotations for configuration. Annotations manifest themselves in a couple of ways. More information, on annotations, including code samples, can be found at http://struts.apache.org/2.x/docs/annotations.html.

Zero Configuration

Zero Configuration provides annotation support to avoid the "action" XML configuration, and if you are always extending from existing packages the "struts.xml" configuration file can be avoided all together. It consists of four class-level annotations, these are:

Annotation	Description
Namespace	A string value of the desired namespace (defined in the "struts.xml" configuration file)
ParentPackage	A string value of the desired parent package
Results	A list of the "Result" annotations
Result	Provides the mapping to the results for the action, there are four attributes: • name – the string result from the action method to configure • type – the class to • value – any value that the result type is expecting, this would be an action name for redirect result type and a JSP for the dispatcher result type • parameters – an array of string parameters

In addition to using these annotations, there is additional configuration that is required. In the filter configuration in web.xml, the packages that are being configured via annotations need to be specified. This is achieved using an "init-param" called "actionPackages", the value being a comma delimited list of packages.

```
<filter>
  <filter-name>struts</filter-name>
  <filter-class>
    org.apache.struts2.dispatcher.FilterDispatcher
  </filter-class>
  <init-param>
    <param-name>actionPackages</param-name>
```

```
    <param-value>
      user.actions,other.actions
    </param-value>
  </init-param>
</filter>
```

Each of these packages, as well as all their sub-packages, will be scanned for classes that implement Action or whose name ends in "Action", and the annotation configuration is added to the runtime configuration. If no namespace annotation is used, the namespace is generated from the package name. This is done by dropping the part of the package name used in the "actionPackages" configuration value. In other words, if "actions" was the "actionPackages" value, and the action being configured is "actions.admin.user.AddAction", then the namespace would be "/admin/user".

Using these annotations doesn't avoid the XML altogether - but it is a great start. Package information such as default interceptor stacks still needs to be configured, as well as package hierarchies.

Lifecycle Callbacks

There are three method-level lifecycle callback annotations, each invoked at a specific time during the processing of an action. The lifecycle callbacks are different from interceptors and action proxies, as they are specific to the action class being invoked instead of a single class that is utilized across many action classes.

Annotation	Description
Before	The method annotated will be invoked before the method that performs the logic for the action.
BeforeResult	The method annotated will be invoked after the method that performs the logic for the action, but before the result is invoked.
After	The method annotated will be invoked after result is invoked, but before the result is returned to the user.

Validation

For each of the XML configured validators, there is a corresponding annotation. Each annotation will have properties similar to those configured via XML. There are also annotations for defining a class as using annotation based validation, configuring custom validators, and to group validations for a property or class.

Annotation Name	XML Equivalent	Description
RequiredFieldValidator	required	Ensures that the property is not null.
RequiredStringValidator	requiredstring	Ensures that a `String` property is not null and not empty.
StringLengthFieldValidator	stringlength	Checks whether a `String` is within a specific length range.
IntRangeFieldValidator	int	Checks whether an `int` property is within a specific range.
DoubleRangeFieldValidator	double	Checks whether a `double` property is within a specific range.
DateRangeFieldValidator	date	Checks whether a `date` property

		is within a specific range.
ExpressionValidator	expression	Evaluates an ONGL expression (which must return a boolean) using the value stack.
FieldExpressionValidator	fieldexpression	Validates a field using an OGNL expression.
EmailValidator	email	Ensures the property is a valid email address.
UrlValidator	url	Ensures that the property is a valid URL.
ConversionError FieldValidator	conversion	Checks whether the there was a conversion error for the property.
RegexFieldValidator	regex	Checks whether the property value matches the regular expression.
VisitorFieldValidator	visitor	The visitor validator defers the validation of a field to

		another validation file specific to the class of the field.
StringRegexValidator	n/a	Checks whether the string property value matches the regular expression.
CustomValidator	n/a	Used to signify that a custom validator is being used.
ValidationParameter	n/a	Used as a parameter within the CustomValidator annotation.
Validation	n/a	Used to signify that the class is using annotation based validation – can be used on interfaces or classes.
Validations	n/a	Used to group together multiple validations for a property or class.

Conversion and Collections

Like the validation annotations, the conversion and collection annotation provide a corresponding annotation for each option that is configured via the "*-conversion.properties" file.

Annotation Name	Description
KeyProperty	Used to specify the property that is to be used as the key.
Key	The class to use for the key of the map.
Element	The class to use for the value/element of the collection, list or map.
CreateIfNull	Determines if the new element should be created if it currently does not exist in the list or map.
Conversion	Used to signify that the class is using annotation based conversion – can be used on interfaces or classes.
TypeConversion	Determine the converter class to use. If used on a collection, a rule of PROPERTY, MAP, KEY, KEY_PROPERTY or ELEMENT can be used to specific exactly which part is to be converted.

Options for View Technologies

As we saw when talking about the core elements, the tag libraries are not only accessible using JSPs, but they can also be used in Velocity and Freemarker templates or extended for other view technologies. As Velocity and Freemarker are first-class citizens with full tag library support, the developer can choose the best view technology for the project.

As an example of the similarities and differences, let's take a look at how the text field tag would be rendered in each view technology. The text field tag is a common form tag – rendering a HTML form element that allows the user to enter text. There are many attributes to this element, but just two will be shown here – the name attribute, which is the name used to reference this element (both in the HTML and the action attribute); and the label attribute, which is used to display a label in front of the text input box.

For JSPs, the tag library needs to be defined before any tags are used. This occurs once at the start of each JSP page, after which the prefix (in this case "s") can be used to reference the tag libraries.

```
<%@taglib prefix="s" uri="/struts-tags" %>

<s:textfield label="Name" name="person.name" />
```

In Freemarker and Velocity there is less structure than with JSP, as there is no concept of tag libraries. Instead, any object that is added into the templates context will be accessible to the page template. The JSP tag libraries are such objects. The HTTP servlet request and response, value stack and the action just executed are also placed in the templates context to be used.

Similarly to JSPs, Freemarker templates use the "s" prefix to reference the JSP tag libraries. Other attributes of the templates are also very similar to HTML – they start with an"<", they end with a "/>", and the attributes are the same. The one difference is that an "@" symbol is used after the initial angled bracket.

```
<@s.textfield label="First Name" name="person.name"/>
```

More information on Freemarker can be found at http://freemarker.sourceforge.net/.

Velocity is much less HTML-like syntax than Freemarker. Each JSP tag name is prefixed with "#s", and the name-value pairs are delimited by double quotes within parenthesis.

```
#stextfield ("label=Name" "name=person.name")
```

More information on Velocity can be found at http://velocity.apache.org/.

As well as JSP, Velocity and Freemarker, XML can be rendered either directly from the action, or via an XSL transformation using the XSLT result type. There is also some interesting work going on that would allow Struts2 to accept form or request input in JSON format, and render output results as JSON format – making Struts2 a flexible server for any type of view technology, or even a combination of view technologies for the same action in the same project.

Know the Provided Tag Libraries and their Features

To provide integration from the user interface back into the action, and to manipulate this information, Struts2 provides various tag libraries that are accessible to JSP, Velocity and Freemarker views.

By default, the value attribute of the form tags and many of the attributes of the other tags accept OGNL expressions. If the attribute you are interested in does not do this by default – for example the "label" attribute – there is a high probability that you can execute expressions by surrounding the expression with the tokens "%{" and "}".

Being able to execute OGNL expressions is a powerful feature, especially since the tag libraries also have access to the value stack with which you can:
- Access named HTTP objects for the application scope, session scope, request scope as well as the attributes and parameters of the request
- Access the action that has just been executed
- Access the model from the action that has just been executed

- Access temporary object – for example the object representing the current loop of the iteration, or perhaps an object that you have placed on the value stack
- Store temporary objects
- Obtain validation issues from the last action executed
- Obtain internationalization text for provided keys
- Make calls to methods of static objects and obtain values of static properties

Up-to-date information regarding the tag libraries can be found at http://struts.apache.org/2.x/docs/tag-reference.html. To get you started, here are the tags from all four categories along with descriptions. Individual attributes of each tag, as well as more detailed usage information, can be found by following the link above.

Those tags marked with an asterisk (*) are either Ajax-based tags, or are able to operate in either an Ajax or non-Ajax mode.

Control Tags

Name	Description
if, elseif & else	These three tags provide flow control logic with the page. The "if" and "elseif" provide a "test" attribute which must contain an OGNL expression that evaluates to a boolean result.
append	Used to append multiple iterators together into a single iterator. Each iterator is specified using a contained "param" tag. All elements from each iterator are added to the resulting iterator in the order specified.
generator	Generates an iterator from a delimited list within a string value. The delimiter character, as well as custom converters

	can be specified.
iterator	Iterate over a collection. Accessing an iterator status object (to provide information about the current loop position) as well as being able to specify the id of the current loop object is possible.
merge	Used to merge multiple iterators together into a single iterator. Each iterator is specified using a contained "param" tag. The resulting iterator has all the first elements, then all the second elements, etc. from each iterator, in turn, in the resulting iterator (in the order specified).
sort	Sorts a collection by a specific comparator. The resulting collection can then be iterated over from within this tag.
subset	Selects a subset of the collection. This can be decided by range, or by providing a custom decider object. The resulting collection can then be iterated over from within this tag.

Data Tags

Name	Description
a*	Renders a HTML link element.
action	Calls an action from within a page, and can be configured to render the results. This tag can be used as a dynamic include, to call a common action to obtain data without rendering a result, or in place of calling actions before the page template.
bean	Instantiates a bean of the specified class and places it on the value stack. Using the contained "param" tag you can set properties on the newly created object.

date	Formats a `Date` object.
debug	Renders information about the value stack for debugging.
i18n	Places additional resource bundles on the stack to use for internationalization text.
include	Makes a call and dynamically includes the result in the current page. Request parameters can be specified using a contained "param" tag.
param	A generic tag used to specify name value pairs, where the value can be static text or specified as an expression obtained via the value stack. This tag is not used by itself, but rather contained as a sub-tag of other tags.
push	Pushes a value on to the value stack.
set	Takes a value from the value stack and sets it as an attribute under a specific HTTP scope (application, session, request, page or action).
text	Retrieves a text value from a resource bundle for a specified key. The "param" tag can be used to specify additional variables from within the resulting text.
url	Generates a valid URL (including the servlet context or any portlet information) assigning it to an id in the value stack.
property	Obtains the value of a property from the value stack. This may be a complex path, and a default value can be specified if the value has not been assigned.

Form Tags

Name	Description
checkbox	Renders a single HTML checkbox element.
checkboxlist	Renders a series of HTML checkbox elements by using a list of objects as the input data.
combobox	Provides combo-box functionality by placing a text HTML input and select HTML input elements together. The user can then either select from the list or enter a new value.
datetimepicker	Renders a HTML drop-down widget that allows the user to select a date / time.
doubleselect	Renders two HTML select elements. Selecting a value from the first list will change the options in the second list.
head	Renders HTML header information, specifically used to include CSS and JavaScript files used in themes.
file	Renders a HTML file input element.
form*	Renders a HTML form element.
hidden	Renders a HTML hidden element.
label	Renders a HTML label, allowing for consistent UI treatments.
optiontransfer select	Renders two HTML select elements with HTML buttons between them. The buttons allowing the user to transfer values between the lists.
optgroup	Creates an option select group with a HTML select element.
password	Renders a HTML password element.
reset	Renders a reset button as either a HTML button or HTML input field.
select	Renders a HTML select element.

| submit* | Renders a HTML submit button or link – could be a HTML input element, and image element or a button element.

When using the default ActionMapper there are four special "name" attribute prefixes for the submit tag that alter the URL, action or method that the form would normally invoke. These are: "method:", "action:", "redirect:" and "redirect-action". Place the method, URL or action to be invoked after the colon in the name. More information can be found at http://struts.apache.org/2.x/docs/actionmapper.html. |
|---|---|
| textarea | Renders a HTML text area element. |
| textfield | Renders a HTML text field element. |
| token | Renders a token that stops the double submission of forms by the user. Works in conjunction with the "token" or "token-session" interceptors. |
| updownselect | Renders a HTML select element along with HTML buttons that move the selected item in the list up or down. When submitted, the list elements will remain in the order that they are arranged. |

Non-Form UI Tags

Name	Description
actionerror	Renders any errors from the action that has just executed.
actionmessage	Renders any messages from the action that has just executed.
component	Renders a custom UI widget.

	Code that is being copied into multiple templates can be extracted into a custom component. The custom component is placed into the target template before rendering starts. Each component can be further customized via "param" tags from each template it is being included from.
div*	Renders a HTML DIV element.
fielderror	Renders any field level errors from the action that has just executed.
tabbedpanel*	Renders a HTML tabbed panel widget.
tree & treenode	Renders a HTML tree widget.

Customize UI Themes

As part of the tag library architecture, each tag has classes that manage the model and the logic, as well as one or more Freemarker templates that control how the element is rendered in HTML. The templates can be utilitarian, providing just the necessary HTML elements or, in the case of the form and non-form UI tag categories, it can provide rich formatting, including data for the form element as well as message and error information.

For the most basic user interface needs, the default layouts may suffice. However, it is more likely that there are more complex requirements that need to be incorporated. With the new layouts you have two options – the HTML can be incorporated into each and every page in the application, or the default theme templates can be modified to provide new themes for the necessary changes. Like extracting visual formatting information into CSS files, creating new themes provides significant maintenance benefits (especially as the number of pages in the application grows).

Creating or modifying a theme is easy. Create a directory called "template" in the root web application directory. Now you have some options.

If you want to create a new theme, create a new directory with the name for the new theme in the "template" directory – for example let's call it "modified". From here, you can start building templates from scratch, or you can copy the templates from the Struts2 distribution and modify them as needed. When you want the tag to use the new "modified" theme rather than the default "xhtml" theme, you will need to change the theme attribute on each and every tag to "modified".

```
<s:textfield label="Name" name="person.name"
    theme="modified" />
```

If you only wish to change certain templates, you can override specific templates only. Create a directory called "xhtml" (this is the default theme in Struts2) in the "template" directory created above. Next, create new templates or modify template from the Struts2 distribution. It is very important to keep the names the same as they are in the Struts2 distribution. As the template is the same name, we are using the same theme as the default, and the web applications "template" directory is searched before the Struts2 JAR file – the modified templates will be used without any further intervention from us.

If you wish to completely replace a theme, modify the "struts.properties" file. In our case, we want the change the "struts.ui.theme" property to our new "modified" theme. There is also an option to change the directory that the theme templates reside in.

```
struts.ui.theme=modified
struts.ui.templateDir=template
```

Use Global Results for Common Outcomes

Results are configured for the outcomes of specific actions, but they can also be defined globally for a package scope. Refactoring out common action results, such as "error" or "logon", as application results allows each action configuration to be streamlined and deal only with those results that are specific to the logic being executed.

The `<result ... />` tag used in the global results has exactly the same form as that used in the action results – with a unique user provided "name" attribute and a "type" attribute to allow for different rendering options. The difference is that the global results tags are placed in a `<global-results ... />` tag under the root `<package ... />` tag.

```
<package ... >

    <global-results>
        <result name="logon">/logon.jsp</result>
        <result name="error">/error.jsp</result>
        ...
    <global-results>

    ...

</package>
```

Once defined in the "struts.xml" configuration file, any action in the application can utilize the result.

Manage Exception Handling Declaratively

When developing web applications, there are several different categories of exceptions that need to be handled. There are those exceptions that are specific to the service or business object being called – these cannot be handled declaratively, and will need to be handled programmatically as normal.

But there are also exceptions that:
- Cannot be handled and need the user to be directed to an error page until the problem is rectified. This is

generally a system level or resource level problem, and not related to the web application logic. An example would be a network problem causing issues connecting to the database.

- Are not logic related problems, but do require the user to be redirected to perform additional tasks. An example would be a security exception being thrown because the user has tried to access a web page without logging on. Once the user has logged on to the system, they can continue without problems.

- Are logic related problems and can be recovered from by modifying the user workflow. This category is usually resource related and would include exceptions related to unique constraint violations, concurrent modification of data or locking problems.

All these exception categories can be handled declaratively without the need to modify actions.

When the exception can be thrown by any action in the web application, it should be defined as a global exception. Global exceptions are placed in a `<global-exception-mappings … />` tag under the `<package … >` tag in the "struts.xml" configuration file.

```
<global-exception-mappings>
    <exception-mapping result="sqlException"
        exception="java.sql.JDBCConnectionException"/>
    <exception-mapping result="unknownException"
        exception="java.lang.Exception"/>
</global-exception-mappings>
```

Under the `<global-exception-mappings … />` tag there can be any number of `<exception-mapping … />` tags. Each mapping has two attributes – an "exception" attribute that defines the package and name of the class of the exception, and the "result" attribute that defines the result to be redirected to.

Each exception mapping is checked in the order that it is configured. Once a matching exception (or a sub-class) is found, processing stops and the request is forwarded to the configured and previously mapped result. Otherwise, the next exception configured is processed for a match.

If the exception is limited to the scope of an action, the same `<exception-mapping … />` tag can be configured within the `<action … />` tag.

```
<action name="my" class="com.fdar.infoq.MyAction" >
    <result>view.jsp</result>
    <interceptor-ref name="basicStack"/>
    <exception-mapping result="exists"
        exception="ConstraintViolationException" />
</action>
```

The attributes of the tag are exactly the same as the global definition. If no matching exception is found for an action level exception mapping, the global mappings are processed for a match.

You will also need to ensure that the "exception" interceptor is in the interceptor stack configured for actions that require declarative exception handling. By default, the "exception" interceptor is included in all interceptor stacks provided in Struts2.

As well as modifying the result that is processed when an exception is thrown, the "exception" interceptor adds two elements to the value stack to provide information about the exception.

Name	Description
exception	The exception object that was thrown.
exceptionStack	The string value of the stack trace.

These values can be used to display the exception stack trace to the user, to display a friendly user message, or even to re-arrange the page layout to allow for additional data entry and then re-submission of a form.

Internationalization

Struts2 provides extensive internationalization support through resource bundles, interceptors and tag libraries. The core functionality is provided via resource bundles, so we'll start our discussion there.

Resource Bundles

Struts2 uses resource bundles to provide multiple language and locale options to the users of the web application. There is no requirement to provide a single monolithic file with all the text from the entire application (although this option is supported by using only a properties file for a common action base). Instead, the properties files for the application can be broken down into manageable sizes.

Properties files named corresponding to the action class (base classes and interfaces) and package scopes, or as arbitrary file names. To find a keys value, the properties files are searched in the following order until the key is found:

1. The properties file for the action class – i.e. MyAction.properties
2. The properties file for each base class in the action hierarchy, all the way up to Object.properties
3. A properties file for each interface and sub-interface
4. If the action is model-driven, a properties file for the model objects class (and each base class, interface and sub-interface for the model class)
5. A properties file called "package.properties" in each package from the action back up to the root package
6. Properties files configured in "struts.properties" under the "struts.custom.i18n.resources" configuration key.

This provides a lot of flexibility.

Interceptors and Determining the Locale

By default, Struts2 will set the users locale for the session from the `HttpServletRequest` object. This comes directly from the web browser, and is based on the Accept-Language HTTP header.

When a web application needs to present content in multiple languages that are not dependant on the locale of the web browser, the "i18n" interceptor can be used. This interceptor checks for a request parameter called "request_locale", and saves this information to the user session. Then, until it is changed by the request parameter again, the specified locale will remain as the locale for the remained of the user's session.

Tag Libraries

Tag libraries are the final piece in the puzzle. All tags support internationalization via locales when it makes sense. For example, the "date" tag uses the users locale to determine the correct formatting for the date; the "actionerror" and "fielderror" tags use the provided keys from the declarative validation configuration to obtain message text to render; as does the "actionmessage" tag. There are a few tags that deserve more detailed attention.

There are two way to programmatically obtain internationalized text for a page, both require the action to extend `ActionSupport` so that the necessary internationalization methods are available. The first is by using the "text" tag, which searches for text for the key provided by the "name" attribute:

```
<s:text name="label.greeting"/>

<s:text name="label.greeting2">
    <s:param >Mr Smith</s:param>
</s:text>
```

Additional information can be provided in the resource bundle values using tokens. The examples above would correspond to the following properties file entries:

```
label.greeting=Hello there!
label.greeting2=Hello there {0}!
```

The second way of obtaining the text values is by using OGNL methods and the "property" tag. The difference between this technique and the previous one is the stylistic choice of the developer[x]. Being a method call, the OGNL expression can be used in any tag that evaluates expressions. Using the same example from above, the JSP would be:

```
<s:property value="getText('label.greeting')"/>

<s:property value="getText('label.greeting2')">
    <s:param >Mr Smith</s:param>
</s:text>
```

Because the "label" attribute is not by default an OGNL expression, we need to use the "%{" and "}" token to force Struts2 to interpret it as an expression.

```
<s:textfield label="%{getText('label.greeting')}"/>
```

If there is a need for large sections of text, OGNL expressions can be used in the "include" tag to specify special language directories. Just make sure that each action extends a base class that exposes a method to determine the locale directory. In this case we have a getLocaleDirectory() method:

```
<s:include
    value="/include/%{localeDirectory}/copyright.html" />
```

The i18n tag provides a way to provide additional resource bundles to the value stack of the page being rendered, the "name" attribute providing the name of the resource bundle. Any tag contained within the "i18n" tag will then have access to the new resource bundle text.

```
<s:i18n name="myCustomBundle">
    The value for abc in myCustomBundle
    is <s:text name="abc"/>
</s:i18n>
```

6

Integrating with Other Technologies

In previous chapters we have covered the techniques for integrating external technologies with Struts2. To recap, here are the techniques:

- *Interceptors* – can change the user's workflow, modified the result and inject objects into the action
- *Result Types* – allows post-processing, and additional result-based processing or rendering of information returned by the action
- *Plug-in packages* – new interceptors, result types, results and actions can be packaged together into a plug-in that can be re-used across many projects
- *Plug-in extensions points* – allows new implementations of the core framework classes to be substituted in to Struts2, thus changing the way the framework behaves

The goal of this chapter is not to describe every and each of the integration options in detail, but rather to provide a brief overview to what types of integrations are possible, how the integration is achieved, some basic configuration information and where to find more information. This chapter is also not intended to provide information on how to use the library used for integration, but assumes that the reader understands the functionality already.

Up-to-date information regarding all integrations (Apache and 3rd party) can be found on the Struts2 wiki at http://cwiki.apache.org/S2PLUGINS/home.html. New projects are constantly being added. If you don't see what you need now, check back in a few months because it might have been added. And if you're adding a new integration to your own web application, consider implementing it as a plug-in and sharing it with others.

Page Decoration and Layout

Developing web applications usually means there is going to be a standard page layout that is used for the entire application, as well as a selection of additional layouts to be used for various modules, pages and wizards. Depending on whether your preference is to specify the layout, or to let the URL specify the layout, you will most likely choose either Struts Tiles[xi] or SiteMesh[xii]. Struts2 provides integrations for both these layout technologies.

SiteMesh

SiteMesh is installed by adding the plug-in[xiii] into your web applications "/WEB-INF/lib" directory or by adding a dependency to your Maven2 "pom.xml" build file:

```
<dependency>
    <groupId>org.apache.struts</groupId>
    <artifactId>struts2-sitemesh-plugin</artifactId>
    <version>2.0.6</version>
</dependency>
```

A servlet filter also needs to be configured. This filter enables access to the value stack from the SiteMesh decorators, and ensures that the `ActionContext` is cleaned up when the decorator has finished (and not before).

```
<filter>
    <filter-name>struts-cleanup</filter-name>
    <filter-class>
        org.apache.struts2.dispatcher.ActionContextCleanUp
    </filter-class>
</filter>
```

If you are using Freemarker or Velocity for page rendering, you will need to add one of these additional filters:

```
<filter>
    <filter-name>sitemesh</filter-name>
    <filter-class>
        org.apache.struts2.sitemesh.FreeMarkerPageFilter
    </filter-class>
</filter>
<filter>
    <filter-name>sitemesh</filter-name>
    <filter-class>
        org.apache.struts2.sitemesh.VelocityPageFilter
    </filter-class>
</filter>
```

Finally, the order of the filter mappings is important. Both the "struts-cleanup" and the "sitemesh" (if used) filter need to be configured before the "struts" (`FilterDispatcher`) filter:

```
<filter-mapping>
    <filter-name>struts-cleanup</filter-name>
    <url-pattern>/*</url-pattern>
</filter-mapping>
<filter-mapping>
    <filter-name>sitemesh</filter-name>
    <url-pattern>/*</url-pattern>
</filter-mapping>
...
<filter-mapping>
    <filter-name>struts</filter-name>
    <url-pattern>/*</url-pattern>
</filter-mapping>
```

The specific decorator files for the web application can now be developed, and configured to match specific URL patterns or metadata in "decorators.xml".

Tiles

Apache Tiles, just like SiteMesh, is installed by adding the plug-in[xiv] into your web applications "/WEB-INF/lib" directory or by adding a dependency to your Maven2 "pom.xml" build file:

```
<dependency>
    <groupId>org.apache.struts</groupId>
    <artifactId>struts2-tiles-plugin</artifactId>
    <version>2.0.6</version>
</dependency>
```

In order to load the tiles configuration, a servlet listener needs to be configured:

```
<listener>
    <listener-class>
        org.apache.struts2.tiles.StrutsTilesListener
    </listener-class>
</listener>
```

The listener loads the "tiles.xml" configuration file, which defines each tile for your application, from the "WEB-INF" directory. Unlike SiteMesh, Tiles are implemented as a new result type. Each action result that wishes to use a Tiles layout needs to provide the attribute "type" with value "tiles" (or alternately set the Tiles result to be the default), and provide the name of the tile to use. The Tile name needs to be defined in the configuration file "tiles.xml".

```
<action name="my" class="com.fdar.infoq.MyAction" >
    <result type="tiles">myaction.layout</result>
</action>
```

Version 2 of Tiles is used in Struts2. This version has not yet had a stable release and could undergo further change. For this reason Tiles support is currently marked as experimental in Struts2.

Business Services / Dependency Injection

The Spring Framework plug-in is the preferred dependency injection (DI) or inversion of control (IoC) container for Struts2, and as such is responsible for providing fully configured business service instances to actions.

There are several options available, each at different levels of stability:

- The Plexus[xv] plug-in is a new addition to the code base, and it is currently marked as experimental. By using a Plexus id, rather than the class name in any of the "struts.xml" configuration file entries, Plexus will create the class instance and inject all dependencies it is aware of. More information of the plug-in can be found at http://cwiki.apache.org/S2PLUGINS/plexus-plugin.html.

- PicoContainer[xvi] is another option for an IoC container and although WebWork provided support, a Struts2 plug-in does not currently exist.
- EJB3, although not an IoC container, is another technology that can be used to provide business services to your actions. EJB3 is currently not supported via plug-ins; however the implementation would be simple. There are three options available – implement a custom `ObjectFactory` to obtain EJB references for actions and install the new factory in your web application using the "struts.objectFactory" property in the "struts.properties" configuration file; create a new interceptor that interrogates each actions and injects an EJB reference as required; or use the Spring framework plug-in to access either JPA or EJBs; a tutorial is provide at http://cwiki.apache.org/S2WIKI/struts-2-spring-jpa-ajax.html.

As the Spring Framework is the preferred library, we are going to focus on it.

Spring Framework

Installing Spring support involves downloading and copying the Spring plug-in[xvii] into your web applications "/WEB-INF/lib" directory or adding the Spring plug-in as a dependency to your Maven2 "pom.xml" build file:

```
<dependency>
    <groupId>org.apache.struts</groupId>
    <artifactId>struts2-spring-plugin</artifactId>
    <version>2.0.6</version>
</dependency>
```

To the "web.xml" configuration file you will need to add two blocks of code. The first registers a listener that enables Spring integration for application objects:

```
<listener>
  <listener-class>
    org.springframework.web.context.ContextLoaderListener
  </listener-class>
</listener>
```

And then the location of the Spring configuration file needs to be specific. In this case, any XML file starting with "applicationContext" will be loaded:

```
<context-param>
    <param-name>contextConfigLocation</param-name>
    <param-value>
        classpath*:applicationContext*.xml
    </param-value>
</context-param>
```

You are now ready to go with Spring support. Any object that needs to be created will be delegated to the Spring object factory. If it knows how to create the object instance it will, otherwise the responsibility will fall back to the framework to create the instance.

For all objects created, whether by the Spring object factory or by Struts2, Spring will be consulted to determine whether it manages any dependant objects. As the default DI container, it will obtain an instance of any dependant objects and set them on the target object instance as necessary. This is especially important for the action class, as the action itself will most likely be created by Struts2 but it will need to have its business services injected by Spring.

Another important factor is how the dependency wiring is determined. For the following class, should Spring inject the bean with an id value of "service" or class type "MyService"?

```
public class MyAction {

    private MyService myService;

    public void setService( MyService service ) {
        myService = service;
    }

    public String execute() {
        ...
    }
}
```

The answer is the id with value "service", but this can be configured. The property in the "struts.properties" file that need to be modified is "struts.objectFactory.spring.autoWire" – by default this value is "name" but there are four options:

Value	Description
name	Spring uses the name / id value in the bean definition to auto-wire the bean.
type	Spring uses the class name in the bean definition to auto-wire the bean.
auto	Spring will determine the best method of wiring the bean.
constructor	Spring will auto-wire via the beans constructor.

There is also a way to have the action completely managed by Spring. This is a more complex configuration, and those that are interested can refer to the Spring plug-in documentation.

Databases

There is nothing special that enables database integration in Struts2, however, there are different ways that database access can be employed:

- *Via Tag Libraries* – since you are using an action based framework this is probably not the best option, but it is possible; data can be accessed directly from JSPs via tag libraries (JSTL or custom libraries) that then format the information

- *Custom DAOs via Dependency Injection* – if you are using dependency inject, you can take advantage of the library to inject in your custom data access objects (DAO) that are required in the action; once the action has a reference to the DAO, it can call the methods as if it had created the instance itself
- *DAO / ORM via Dependency Injection* – if you are taking advantage of advanced DAO or ORM libraries (such as iBatis or Hibernate) you should invest in utilizing a fully-features dependency injection framework such as Spring; Spring provides everything necessary to configure and initialize many different DAO and ORM libraries, requiring very little from the actions; when the action is ready for the business logic to be executed, all the necessary data access object instances are ready to go
- *Accessed Indirectly via Business Services* – instead of accessing the data access object directly, the calls are made indirectly via business services; the business service, like the previous options, are injected into the action by the dependency injection framework

As a side note, if you are thinking about utilizing Hibernate as an ORM technology on your project, investigate the "OpenSessionInView" filter or interceptor. Having the Hibernate session open until the rendering of the JSP is complete allows Hibernate to perform lazy-loading fetches to the database successfully. Otherwise, the action or business service or DAO would need to pre-fetch all the collections that the JSP needs ahead of time.

Security

Like database integration, there is nothing special that provides security integration in Struts2. It is up to the application architect or developer to decide at which layers in the infrastructure or application authorization and authentication occur.

Authentication can occur:

- *External to the application* – an example would be a single sign-on (SSO) server or authentication modules provided by the application server
- *Within the application* – via a HTML form or another type of challenge-response mechanism

Authorization can occur:

- *At the URI level* – each URI that is requested is matched against the user credentials (that made the request) to see if they are allowed access
- *At the sub-page level* – there may be certain sections of a page can only be viewed, modified or have action performed for particular access levels
- *At the action level* – each action may be required to determine access levels before performing business operations or logic
- *At the business service level* – each method on a business service may be required to determine access levels before performing logic
- *At the domain object or database level* – for a generic method call to obtain data or domain objects, different results could be returned depending on the callers' access level

From the perspective of a Struts2 web application, the user is authenticated to access the URL or not. Once the user is allowed to access the application, there are a couple of options.

The first is that an external solution provides the users' credentials via the `HttpServletRequest` object. From here, the username and as well the users role information can be accessed at the action level (by implementing the `PrincipalAware` interface and configuring the "servlet-config" on the interceptor stack) and exposed from the action to the page being rendered. Existing Struts2 tags can then be used to limit access depending on roles.

Next, is that the users' credentials to the `HttpServletRequest` haven't been populated. In this case an interceptor needs to be developed to authenticate and obtain the necessary role information, and to populate the information. This may be as complex as developing the logon form, logon and logoff code, authentication logic, etc., or it may be as simple as obtaining the information from an exposed API and setting it on the action.

The last case is when a 3rd party solution does everything for you. An example would be the acegi project. Acegi provides everything that is needed to secure a web application –servlet filters, custom tag libraries, and integration into Spring for securing business objects as well as domain objects – and all completely external to the Struts2 web application. Integration would only be necessary if the authorization information is required during the processing of the action. In this case, an interceptor could be paired with an action interface to supply the `Authz` instance to the action. More details on this approach can be found at http://struts.apache.org/2.x/docs/can-we-use-acegi-security-with-the-framework.html.

Although not related to 3rd party security integration, one security concern in using Struts2 is that any action has access to any object within the Value Stack. This assumption may not always be correct. To designate specific Value Stack objects that are allowed or blocked from an action, you can configure and utilize the `com.opensymphony.xwork2.interceptor.ParameterFilterInterceptor` interceptor (this interceptor is not currently configured like the others that were discussed in the previous chapter). More information on the configuration is contained in the JavaDoc for the interceptor.

Ajax

The Ajax support in Struts2 has been a little tumultuous of late. There is a lot going on, and it's going to take a while for the dust to settle.

At the most basic level, any action can perform as a data server. A request made to a URI can result in a HTML fragment (to be rendered directly in to a DIV), an XML document (via the XSLT result type) or a JSON document (by tweaking the JSP to JSON rather than HTML) that are then processed by JavaScript at the web browser. This is by far the most solid from an implementation standpoint, and is of production quality.

Following this same concept there are three projects to keep and eye on. These are all fairly new, and will take time to mature.

- To automate some of the work needed to provide JSON results, there is the JSON plug-in project – this is a 3rd party plug-in and can be found at
  http://cwiki.apache.org/S2PLUGINS/2007/01/11/json-plugin.html
- Providing interoperability between the Google Web Toolkit (GWT) and Struts2 as a back end data source is the GWT plug-in project –
  http://cwiki.apache.org/S2PLUGINS/2007/01/10/gwt-plugin.html
- Direct web remoting (DWR) has recently added support for remote WebWork2 action invocation using their framework; WebWork2 is the predecessor of Struts2, so all the techniques should be applicable; more information can be found at
  http://getahead.ltd.uk/dwr/server/webwork

Struts2 also provides tag libraries with Ajax functionality, these are:

- *a / link tag* – make a remote call to the server using Ajax
- *form* – provides Ajax-based validation for the form fields (using DWR), and provides the ability to submit the form remotely via Ajax

- *submit* – used in conjunction with a Ajax based form submit
- *div* – obtain the content for a DIV via an Ajax remote call
- *tabbedpanel* – the content for each panel of the tabbed panel is obtained via a Ajax remote call

The underlying implementations of the tags use the dojo library, and some of the tags are making the move from a combination custom JavaScript and dojo implantation to a pure dojo implementation. In the near future, the Ajax tags will be moving into a plug-in. This will allow for different implementation based on different Ajax libraries, which has been requested for some time now.

For all these reasons, the Ajax tag libraries are currently marked as experimental.

About the Author

Ian Roughley is a speaker, writer and independent consultant based out of Boston, MA. For over 10 years he has been providing architecture, development, process improvement and mentoring services to clients ranging in size from fortune 10 companies to start-ups. His professional background includes work in the financial, insurance, pharmaceutical, retail, e-learning, hospitality and supply-chain industries.

Focused on a pragmatic and results-based approach, he is a proponent for open source, as well as process and quality improvements through agile development techniques. Ian is a committer to the WebWork project; member of the Apache Struts PMC; and speaker at No Fluff Just Stuff Symposiums. He is also a Sun Certified Java Programmer and J2EE Enterprise Architect; and an IBM Certified Solutions Architect.

End Notes

i. http://struts.apache.org/2.x

ii. Don Brown, the lead on the Struts Ti project, has more information on the history at
http://www.oreillynet.com/onjava/blog/2006/10/my_history_of_struts_2.html

iii. A list of different open source web frameworks can be found at
http://www.java-source.net/open-source/web-frameworks.

iv. Specifically the property to change this value is "struts.action.extension".

v. Martin Fowler has a thorough explanation of dependency injection at
http://www.martinfowler.com/articles/injection.html

vi. Technically there are four themes – with the fourth being the "ajax" theme.
It has been decided to remove the Ajax functionality from the core Struts2
framework into a plug-in in the next version, and for this reason it will not be
discussed in this section

vii. Swingwork can be found at https://swingwork.dev.java.net/. There is no
longer active development on the project.

viii. For more information see http://www.jmock.org

ix. Documentation for the config browser plug-in can be found at
http://struts.apache.org/2.x/docs/config-browser-plugin.html

x. This is generally true however, using the property tag, the developer would
be able to access the Value Stack and obtain the internationalized text for a
key name that is not known at development time.

xi. http://tiles.apache.org

xii. http://www.opensymphony.com/sitemesh

xiii. http://cwiki.apache.org/S2PLUGINS/sitemesh-plugin.html

xiv. http://cwiki.apache.org/S2PLUGINS/tiles-plugin.html

xv. http://plexus.codehaus.org

xvi. http://picocontainer.codehaus.org

xvii. http://cwiki.apache.org/S2PLUGINS/spring-plugin.html

www.ingramcontent.com/pod-product-compliance
Lightning Source LLC
Chambersburg PA
CBHW051252050326
40689CB00007B/1164